THE AMAZING SPIDER-MAN™

COMING HOME

Reader Services

CUSTOMER SERVICE IN THE UK AND REPUBLIC OF IRELAND
How to continue your collection:
Customers can either place an order with their newsagent or receive issues on subscription.
Back issues: Either order through your newsagent or write to: Marvel Collection, Jacklin Enterprises UK, PO Box 77, Jarrow, NE32 3YH, enclosing payment of the cover price plus £1.00 p&p per copy. (Republic of Ireland: cover price plus €1.75).
Subscriptions: You can have your issues sent directly to your home. For details, see insert in issue 1 or phone our Customer Service Hotline on 0871 472 4240 (Monday to Friday, 9am-5pm, calls cost 10p per minute from UK landline). Alternatively you can write to Marvel Collection, Jacklin Enterprises UK, PO Box 77, Jarrow, NE32 3YH, or fax your enquiries to 0871 472 4241, or e-mail: marvelcollection@jacklinservice.com or visit www.graphicnovelcollection.com

CUSTOMER SERVICE IN OVERSEAS MARKETS

Australia: Back issues can be ordered from your newsagent. Alternatively telephone (03) 9872 4000 or write to:
Back Issues Department, Bissett Magazine Services, PO Box 3460, Nunawading Vic 3131. Please enclose payment of the cover price, plus A$2.49 (inc. GST) per issue postage and handling. Back issues are subject to availability.
Subscriptions: You can have your issues sent directly to your home. For details, see insert in issue 1 or phone our Customer Service Hotline on (03) 9872 4000. Alternatively you can write to Hachette subs offer, Bissett Magazine Services, PO Box 3460, Nunawading Vic 3131, or fax your enquiries to (03) 9873 4988, or order online at www.bissettmags.com.au

New Zealand: For back issues, ask your local magazine retailer or write to: Netlink, PO Box 47906, Ponsonby, Auckland.
South Africa: Back issues are available through your local CNA store or other newsagent.
Subscriptions: call (011) 265 4309, fax (011) 314 2984, or write to: Marvel Collection, Private Bag 10, Centurion 0046 or e-mail: service@jacklin.co.za
Malta: Back issues are only available through your local newsagent.
Malaysia: Call (03) 8023 3260, or e-mail: sales@allscript.com
Singapore: Call (65) 287 7090, or e-mail: sales@allscript.com

Published by Hachette Partworks Ltd, Jordan House,
47 Brunswick Place, London, N1 6EB
www.hachettepartworks.co.uk

Distributed in the UK and Republic of Ireland by Marketforce

This special edition published in 2012 by Hachette Partworks Ltd. forming part of The Ultimate Marvel Graphic Novel Collection.

Printed in Spain.
ISBN: 978-1-906965-94-5

J. MICHAEL STRACZYNSKI
WRITER

JOHN ROMITA JR.
PENCILS

SCOTT HANNA
INKS

DAN KEMP & AVALON STUDIOS
COLOURS

COMICRAFT
LETTERS

AXEL ALONSO
EDITOR

JOE QUESADA
EDITOR IN CHIEF

J. SCOTT CAMPBELL & TIM TOWNSEND
COVER ART

THE AMAZING SPIDER-MAN: COMING HOME

Marco M. Lupoi
Panini Publishing Director (Europe)

Welcome to the very first issue of the Official ***Marvel Graphic Novels Collection***. In the coming books, you'll be treated to the very best stories from the *House of Ideas* covering all of the major story arcs from the 80s to the present day. These include some of my personal favourites that are, in my opinion, absolutely essential for anyone with even a passing interest in comic books or graphic novels, real classics of visual storytelling and great introductions to the fictional universe of Spider-Man, Thor, X-Men and their "marvelous" friends. Kicking off the ground-breaking J. Michael Straczynski/John Romita Jr. run, ***The Amazing Spider-Man: Coming Home*** ushered in a new era to the webbed-wonder's history, bringing something different to Spidey's past - a mythical element to the character that had never been attempted before. This was the first major new story arc of Amazing Spider-Man this century, which gave back to the character much of his gravitas and dramatic flair, in a fight to the finish reminiscent of some of Marvel's greatest classics.
So read on, fasten your seatbelts and enjoy the ride!

Contains material originally published in magazine form as THE AMAZING SPIDER-MAN #30-35. Senior Editor (Hachette Partworks Ltd.), Sarah Gale. Packaged by Panini Publishing, a division of Panini UK Limited. Mike Riddell, Managing Director. Alan O'Keefe, Managing Editor. Simon Frith, Senior Editor. Ed Hammond, Editor. Marco M. Lupoi, Publishing Director Europe.
Tim Warran-Smith, Designer. Additional content: Mike Conroy. Office of publication: Brockbourne House, 77 Mount Ephraim, Tunbridge Wells, Kent TN4 8BS.

THE STORY SO FAR...

Events leading up to Amazing Spider-Man: Coming Home

Following the defeat of his archenemy the Green Goblin, Peter Parker decides to quit being Spider-Man, in order to have a normal life with his beautiful, supermodel wife, Mary Jane. However, it is not long before Peter is forced to pick up his webs once again and become Spider-Man.

This decision to resume his Super Hero activities puts his marriage to Mary Jane under a great deal of stress. To make matters worse, a mysterious stranger begins to stalk MJ. After a battle with the Sinister Six, Peter returns home to find that MJ has left for the airport on a modelling assignment. Disaster strikes, when MJ's plane explodes in mid-air.

Despite mounting evidence that MJ is dead, Peter refuses to accept his wife's demise. As Spider-Man, he searches far and wide to find evidence that she is still alive - even travelling to Latveria, the domain of Doctor Doom. Unfortunately, the web-slinger is unsuccessful in discovering the location of his missing wife.

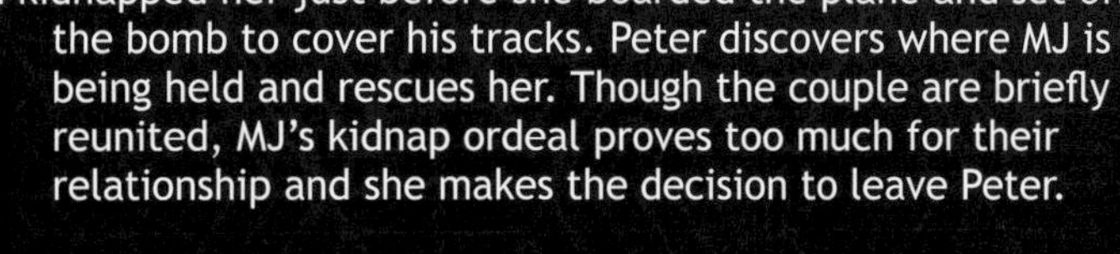

Just as he begins to accept her death, Peter learns that his wife is still alive. MJ's stalker had kidnapped her just before she boarded the plane and set off the bomb to cover his tracks. Peter discovers where MJ is being held and rescues her. Though the couple are briefly reunited, MJ's kidnap ordeal proves too much for their relationship and she makes the decision to leave Peter.

The Amazing Spider-Man #30

COVER ARTWORK

At a demonstration on Radiation, high school student Peter Parker was bitten by an Irradiated Spider from which he gained the Arachnid's Incredible Abilities. When a burglar killed his beloved Uncle Ben, a grief-stricken Peter vowed to use his Great Powers in the service of his fellow man, because he learned an invaluable lesson: With Great Power there must also come Great Responsibility.

Stan Lee Presents: **THE AMAZING SPIDER-MAN**

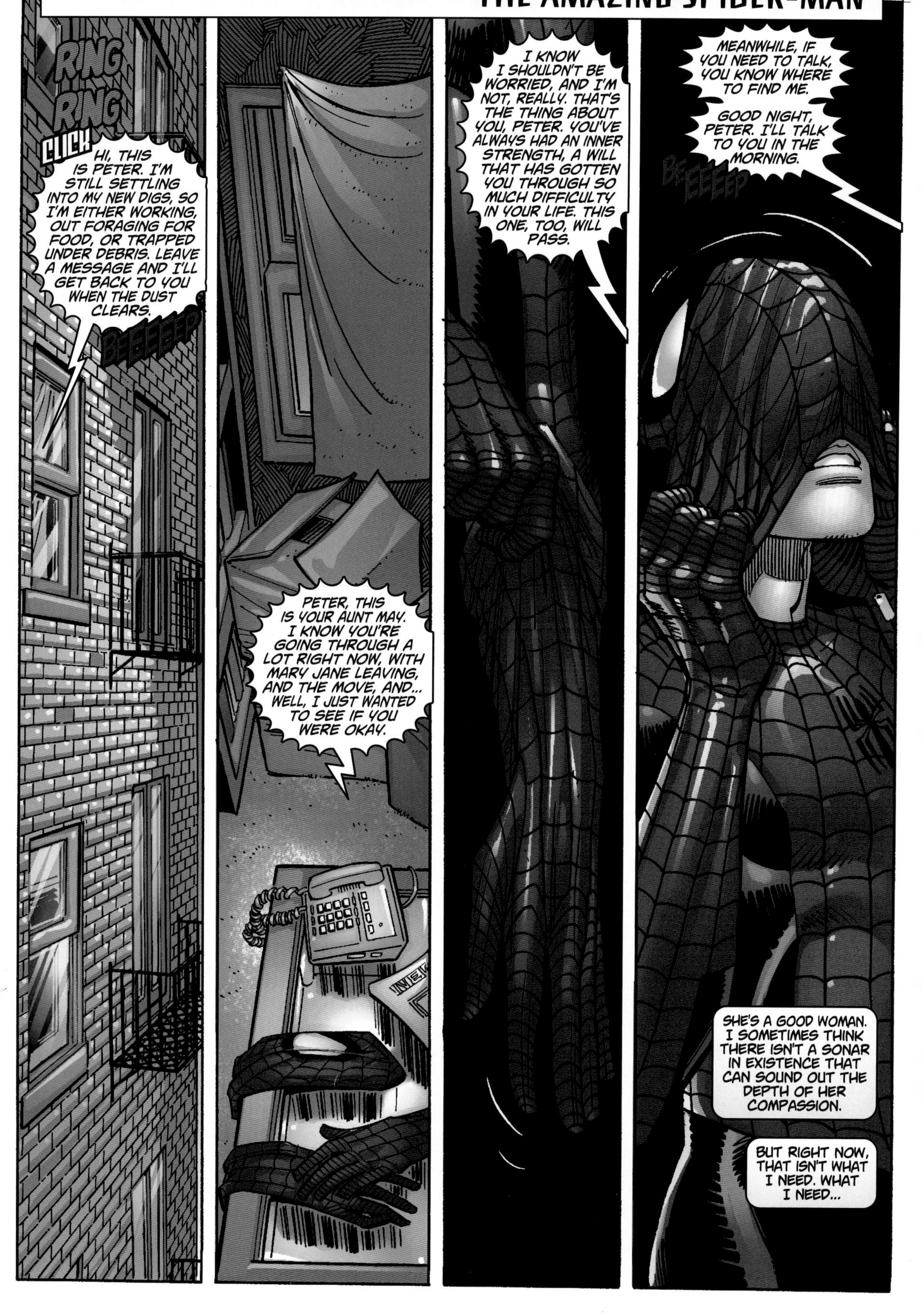

...IS TO GET AWAY AND UP AND OUT.

JUST...OUT. I DON'T EVEN CARE WHERE I GO. I JUST WANT TO...GO.
AND I'M NOT GONNA STOP UNTIL I GET TIRED.

UNFORTUNATELY, IT TAKES A REAL *LONG* TIME FOR ME TO GET TIRED.
BY THAT TIME, I COULD BE IN NEW JERSEY.

AND I DON'T EVEN *KNOW* ANYBODY IN NEW JERSEY...

...AND HERE'S ANOTHER THING.
WHEN I DESIGNED THIS SUIT, WHY THE HECK DIDN'T I DESIGN IT WITH POCKETS? ANYTHING I CARRY, I GOTTA CARRY IT IN A WEB-POUCH. THE FF HAVE POCKETS IN THEIR UNIFORMS. REED RICHARDS' ALONE ARE HUGE.
SCHEDULED FOR DEMOLITION
SQUATTERS WILL BE PROSECUTED!
ROCCO DEMO
ROCCO DEMO
BUT THAT'S BECAUSE HE HAS TO CARRY TRANS-DIMENSIONAL MEGADOODADS AND WHIRLYDOOS IN THEM.
OR MAYBE HE'S JUST REAL HAPPY TO SEE SUE.

'COURSE, IF I HAD POCKETS, STUFF WOULD FALL OUT OF THEM EVERY TIME I DID THIS. OKAY, SO MAYBE I COULD HAVE POCKETS WITH ZIPPERS. MAYBE VELCRO.
YEAH, THAT'D WORK... I'D BE CREEPING UP BEHIND SOMEBODY, AND HAVE TO GET SOMETHING OUT... ZZZZZZZZZZZZIP!

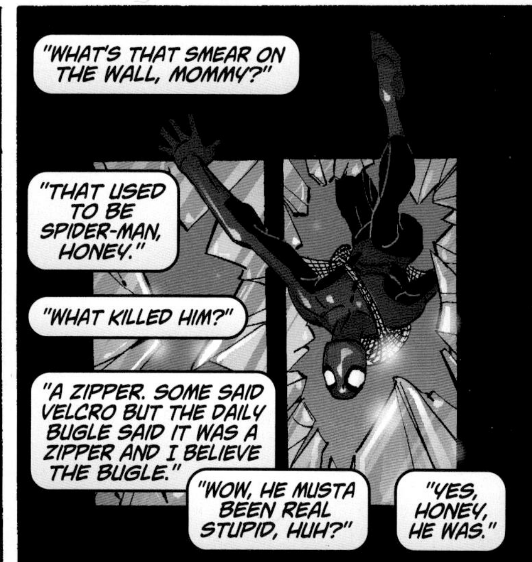
"WHAT'S THAT SMEAR ON THE WALL, MOMMY?"
"THAT USED TO BE SPIDER-MAN, HONEY."
"WHAT KILLED HIM?"
"A ZIPPER. SOME SAID VELCRO BUT THE DAILY BUGLE SAID IT WAS A ZIPPER AND I BELIEVE THE BUGLE."
"WOW, HE MUSTA BEEN REAL STUPID, HUH?"
"YES, HONEY, HE WAS."

-SIGH-
AND WHY THE HECK AM I THINKING ABOUT POCKETS ANYWAY?
BECAUSE IT'S EASIER THAN THINKING ABOUT MY LIFE LATELY?

AND WHY SHOULD THAT BOTHER YOU, PETER?

OH, NO REASON.

EVERYTHING'S FINE.
EVERYTHING'S JUST DUCKY.
EXCEPT THAT WHENEVER I'M REALLY BUGGED ABOUT SOMETHING AND I REALLY NEED TO GO POUND A BAD GUY THERE'S NEVER A BAD GUY AROUND, BUT WHENEVER I'M IN A REALLY GOOD MOOD -- YEAH, LIKE THAT HAPPENS MORE THAN TWICE A YEAR -- THERE'S ALWAYS FOUR OR FIVE BAD GUYS, OR A SINISTER SIX, OR SEVEN, OR NINETEEN WAITING TO BUST MY CHOPS AND RUIN MY DAY AND...

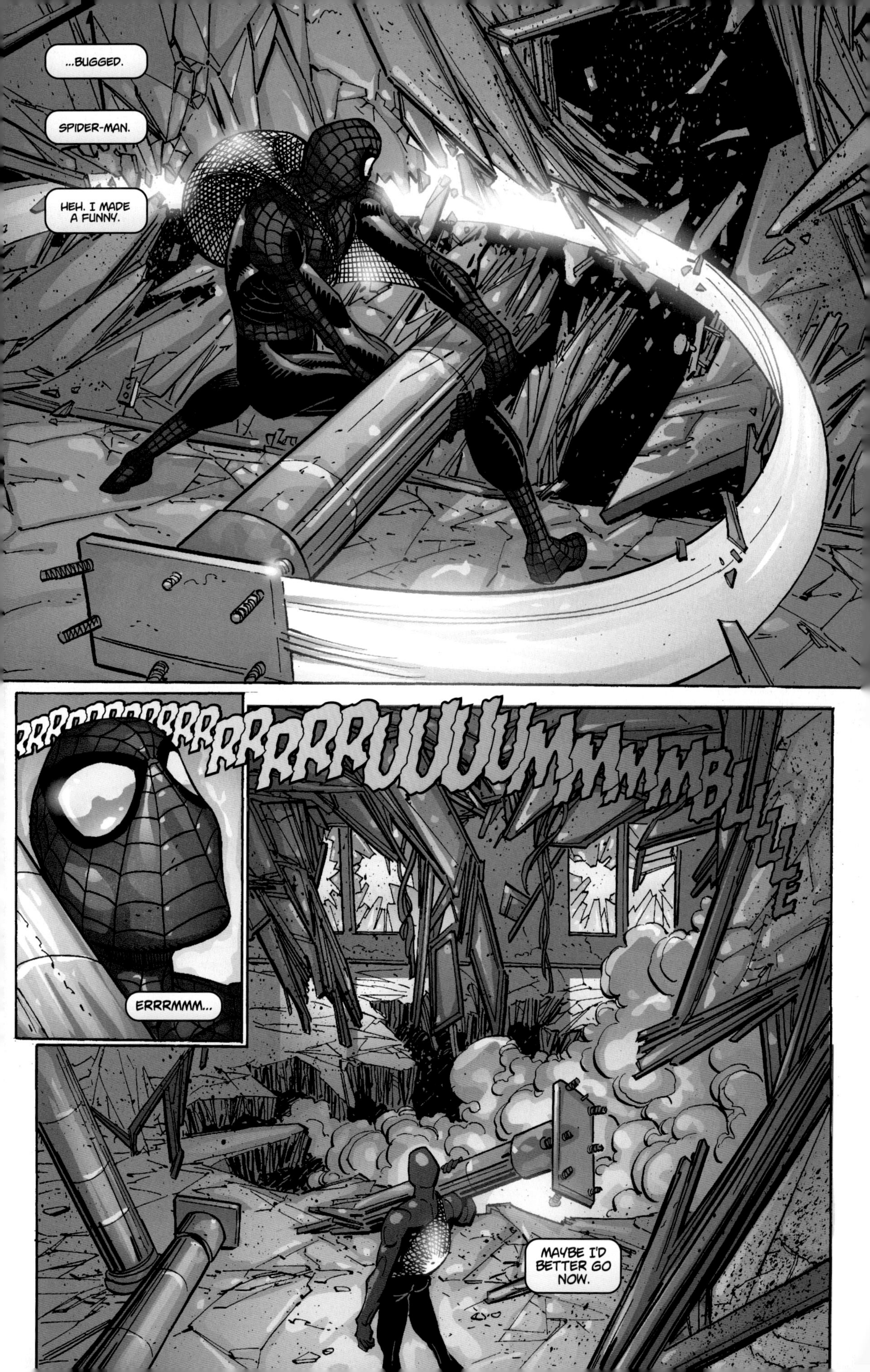
...BUGGED.
SPIDER-MAN.
HEH. I MADE A FUNNY.
RRRRRRRRRRRRRRRRUUUUMMMMMBLLLE
ERRRMMM...
MAYBE I'D BETTER GO NOW.

ALL RIGHT, GET THAT CRANE OVER HERE, WE GOT SIX HOURS TO TEAR THIS PLACE TO --
ROCCO DEMO'S

RRRRRUUMMMBLLE
ROCCO DEM

TINK
TINK TINK

OKAY, LUNCH!

DINER
I DECIDE I NEED SOMETHING TO EAT. SO I PICK A PLACE PRETTY MUCH BY INSTINCT. I'M NOT THINKING ABOUT IT.

AND MAYBE THAT'S WHY I ENDED UP THERE. I WASN'T THINKING. I WAS FEELING.

FOR SOME OF THE MOST IMPORTANT YEARS OF MY LIFE, THIS PART OF TOWN WAS MY HOME.
ANNOYING AS THAT SOMETIMES WAS.
HEY, PARKER! YOU GONNA ACTUALLY **EAT** THAT BURGER? IT'S GOT MORE GRISTLE IN IT THAN **YOU** DO!
HAW-HAW!
YOU GUYS ARE **SUCH** JERKS.

THE FIRST FEW YEARS I CAME TO THIS SCHOOL, I WAS THE SAME AS EVERYBODY ELSE.
4 STAR DINER
ELMER
7

JUST ONE MORE HIGH SCHOOL STUDENT TRYING NOT TO BE NOTICED, NOT TO LOOK WEIRD, WORRIED THAT HE'D NEVER FIT IN.

JOHNS
13
THEN ONE DAY, A SPIDER-BITE MADE SURE I WAS NOTICED, AND THAT I **WOULD** NEVER FIT IN **ANY**WHERE, EVER AGAIN.
SOME THINGS HAVEN'T CHANGED.

BUT THIS PLACE SURE HAS.
HEY! WATCH WHERE YOU'RE WALKING!
P.S. 108
YEAH, WATCH IT, JERKFACE!
AWK --!
LOOK, JUST... CUT IT OUT, OKAY? I DIDN'T DO ANYTHING TO YOU.
YEAH, BUT WE'RE GONNA DO SOMETHING TO YOU, YOU STUPID --
I WOULDN'T ADVISE THAT, GUYS.
THAT SO? WHAT'RE YOU GONNA DO ABOUT IT?
YEAH, YOU'RE NOT A TEACHER, YOU'RE NOT A COP, YOU CAN'T DO SQUAT, MISTER...YOU EVEN TOUCH ME AND I'LL YELL FOR THE COPS AND THEY'LL HAUL YOUR SORRY BUTT TO JAIL, BUDDY, SO JUST TAKE OFF, OKAY?!
JERK!
SEE YOU LATER, JOEY, WHEN YOUR BIG BROTHER AIN'T THERE TO PROTECT YOU.
YOU OKAY?

NO, I'M NOT OKAY... 'CAUSE NOW THEY'RE JUST GONNA GET ME TWICE AS BAD LATER --
-- AND I HATE THEM AND I HATE MY LIFE AND THIS SUCKS AND YOU MADE EVERYTHING WORSE AND I GOTTA GET TO CLASS...
B.R.B.
P.S. 108

I... I MEAN... I'M SORRY, I --
I SAW WHAT HAPPENED THERE, BUDDY.
EXIT

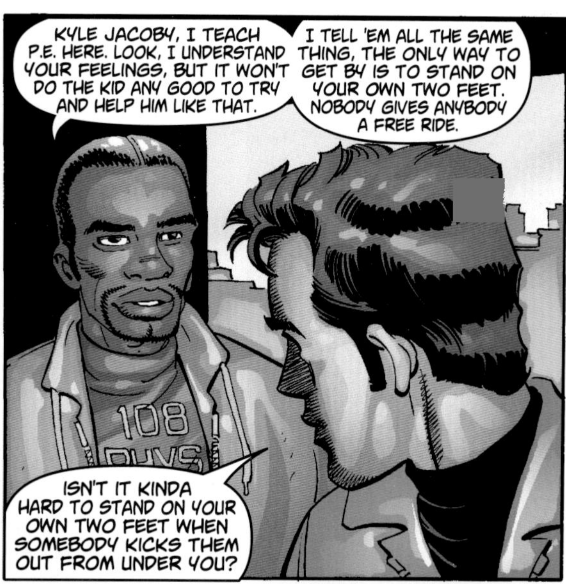
KYLE JACOBY, I TEACH P.E. HERE. LOOK, I UNDERSTAND YOUR FEELINGS, BUT IT WON'T DO THE KID ANY GOOD TO TRY AND HELP HIM LIKE THAT.
I TELL 'EM ALL THE SAME THING, THE ONLY WAY TO GET BY IS TO STAND ON YOUR OWN TWO FEET. NOBODY GIVES ANYBODY A FREE RIDE.
ISN'T IT KINDA HARD TO STAND ON YOUR OWN TWO FEET WHEN SOMEBODY KICKS THEM OUT FROM UNDER YOU?

BUDDY, THERE'S ALWAYS SOMEBODY TRYING TO KICK YOUR FEET OUT FROM UNDER YOU. YOU JUST GOTTA KICK FIRST. JOEY'S GOTTA LEARN THAT FOR HIMSELF.
EVOLVE OR DIE, YOU KNOW?

ESPECIALLY IN A DUMP LIKE THIS. IT WAS QUITE A PLACE ONCE. BUT THINGS CHANGE, YOU KNOW?

HE'S RIGHT. SOME THINGS CHANGE.
BUT SOME THINGS NEVER CHANGE.
UNLESS SOMEBODY MAKES THEM CHANGE.

NOW, I'M NOT SAYING I'M THE KIND OF GUY WHO CARRIES A GRUDGE. FAR BE IT FOR ME TO EVER CARRY A GRUDGE.

BUT I FIGURE, YOU HANG OUT LONG ENOUGH, YOU WATCH SOME PEOPLE, OH, I DUNNO, RANDOMLY...AND SONOVAGUN, AN OPPORTUNITY PRESENTS ITSELF FOR THE UNIVERSE TO BALANCE THINGS OUT.
AS SOMEBODY ONCE SAID, CHANCE FAVORS THE PREPARED MIND.
HOGWA

C'MON MAN, WE AIN'T GOT ALL DAY.
JUST A SEC, I ALMOST GOT IT --

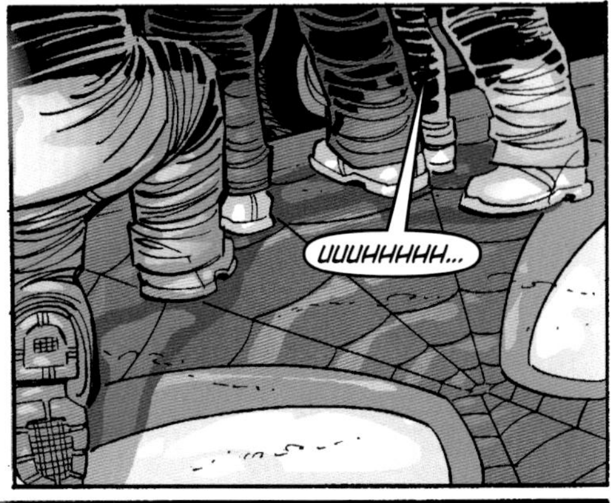
UUUHHHHH...

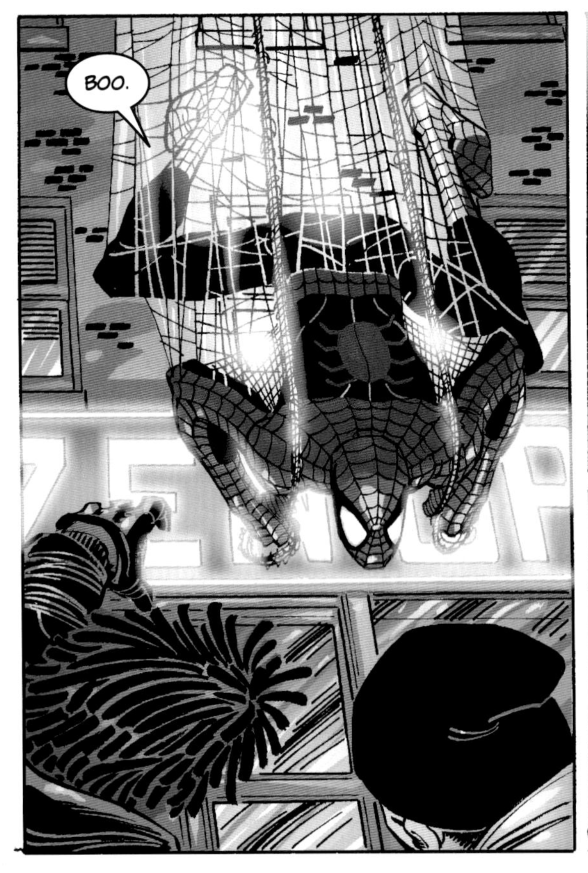
BOO.

AAAAAGGGGHHHHH!
SLOW DOWN! I CAN'T KEEP UP! AWK!
JEEZ, MAN, I WET 'EM, SLOW DOWN...
MAURO

THAT'S ONE SMALL STEP FOR A SPIDER, ONE GIANT LEAP FOR GEEK-KIND...
I SUPPOSE YOU'RE FEELING RATHER PROUD OF YOURSELF RIGHT NOW.

UNDERSTANDABLE. I WOULD, TOO. EVEN IF IT IS A WASTE OF A NICE NIGHT. AND YOUR TALENT.
PETER.
FOR A MOMENT, I'M TOO STUNNED TO TALK. IT ISN'T JUST THAT HE SNUCK UP BEHIND ME, AND WITH MY SPIDER-SENSE THAT'S NOT POSSIBLE.
IT ISN'T EVEN THAT HE CALLED ME PETER, WHICH MEANS HE KNOWS WHO I AM AND THIS COULD SCREW UP MY ENTIRE LIFE.
IT'S THAT HE'S STICKING TO THE WALL SAME AS ME.
I KNOW WHAT YOU'RE THINKING.
WELL, METAPHORICALLY, ANYWAY.
AM I A FRIEND, OR AN ENEMY?
HEY!

JUST A SECOND, LET ME GET MY SHOES ON. I HATE WALKING AROUND BAREFOOT.
HE'S AT LEAST TWICE MY AGE, BUT HE'S FAST. IMPOSSIBLY FAST.
AS FAST AS I AM.

WHO ARE YOU?
I WAS ABOUT TO ASK YOU THE SAME QUESTION.
BUT YOU JUST SAID --
OH, I KNOW YOU'RE PETER PARKER, BUT THAT'S NOT WHO YOU ARE.

LOOK, BUDDY, I'M NOT SAYING YOU'RE RIGHT OR WRONG, BUT DO YOU MIND NOT ANNOUNCING THAT SO LOUD?
RIGHT. SORRY. SECRET IDENTITY AND ALL THAT. SOMETIMES I FORGET.
NOW WHO THE HELL ARE --
MY NAME IS EZEKIEL. AND I HAVE A QUESTION FOR YOU.

DO YOU KNOW WHY PEOPLE USE THE EXPRESSION, "AS DANGEROUS AS GIVING A LOADED GUN TO A SMALL CHILD"?
IT'S NOT BECAUSE THE CHILD IS ESPECIALLY MALICIOUS, OR BECAUSE HE WANTS TO KNOCK OVER A BANK.
IT IS BECAUSE THE CHILD DOES NOT COMPREHEND THE POWER HE HOLDS IN HIS HANDS.

AND NEITHER DO YOU.

LET'S ROMP SOME MORE. I HAVEN'T DONE THIS IN YEARS.
DARN, THERE GO MY SHOES AGAIN...
I KEEP AFTER HIM, DETERMINED NOT TO LET HIM GET AWAY... PLAYING IT QUIET, TO FIND OUT WHAT HE'S AFTER.
IT'S STRANGE, THOUGH... WHEN HE SAID MY NAME, MY GUT TIGHTENED INTO SOMETHING COLD AND SCARED, AND YET...
...AND YET I SENSE NOTHING EVIL IN HIM. HE SEEMS...ALMOST JOYFUL.
CAREFUL, THERE'S A RUSTY NAIL OVER HERE.
LET ME ASK YOU A QUESTION, PE-- ER, SPIDER-MAN. AND DON'T LIE. I'LL KNOW IF YOU LIE.
HOW DID YOU GET YOUR POWERS?
I...
HE KNOWS WHO I AM. THERE'S NO END OF DAMAGE HE COULD DO WITH THAT INFORMATION. I HAVE TO PLAY ALONG. AND IT'S NOT LIKE HE CAN DO ANYTHING WITH THE INFORMATION.
I WAS BITTEN BY A RADIOACTIVE SPIDER.
AHA!
THAT'S WHAT I THOUGHT. THAT EXPLAINS WHY YOU'VE HANDLED IT THIS WAY. NOW HERE'S ANOTHER QUESTION FOR YOU.
LOOK, I'VE JUST ABOUT HAD IT WITH --
NO, WAIT, YOU'LL LIKE THIS ONE, TRUST ME.

DID YOU PERFORM AN AUTOPSY ON THE SPIDER?
NO. IT GOT PRETTY MUCH SMASHED.
HAD YOU EVER SEEN THE SPIDER BEFORE?
NO. NOW LOOK...
THERE ARE THREE STEPS IN KNOWLEDGE. THERE'S WHAT WE THINK, WHAT WE KNOW, AND WHAT WE CAN PROVE.
YOU THINK YOU GOT YOUR POWERS FROM A RADIOACTIVE SPIDER-BITE, AND YOU MAY BELIEVE YOU KNOW IT TO BE TRUE, BUT CAN YOU PROVE IT?
YOU THINK I GOT THESE POWERS AND THIS SUIT AT THE BOTTOM OF A BOX OF CRACKERJACKS? IT HAPPENED RIGHT AFTER I GOT BIT.
YOU'RE STILL MISSING THE POINT.
THIS IS THE POINT. THIS IS THE FIVE MILLION DOLLAR QUESTION. I'M ABOUT TO YANK YOUR CHAIN LIKE NOBODY ELSE EVER HAS BEFORE, AND NOBODY EVER WILL AGAIN. SO LISTEN CAREFULLY.
DID THE RADIATION ENABLE THE SPIDER TO GIVE YOU THESE POWERS?
OR WAS THE SPIDER TRYING TO GIVE YOU THOSE POWERS BEFORE THE RADIATION KILLED IT?
WHICH CAME FIRST? THE RADIATION? OR THE POWER? THE CHICKEN OR THE EGG OR THE POWER?

I...
THE QUESTION HITS ME LIKE A PUNCH IN THE STOMACH. ALL THESE YEARS, AND I HAD NEVER CONSIDERED THAT POSSIBILITY. I'D NEVER EVEN THOUGHT ABOUT IT. I'D JUST ASSUMED. I...
...I DON'T KNOW.

AND THAT'S A GOOD START FOR TONIGHT.

TAKE CARE OF YOURSELF, P. I'LL BE IN TOUCH.
HEY! STOP! WAIT, I --

AND HE'S GONE. NOBODY PULLS A FAST FADE LIKE THAT.
NOBODY BUT ME.

WHO ARE YOU? WHY ARE YOU COMING TO ME WITH ALL THIS NOW?
WHAT DO YOU WANT FROM ME?
I CAME NOW BECAUSE NOW IS THE RIGHT TIME. BECAUSE YOU NEED TO UNDERSTAND.
BECAUSE UNDERSTANDING IS THE ONLY THING THAT MAY HELP YOU SURVIVE WHAT'S COMING.
AND THAT'S AN AWFULLY BIG MAY, P.

AND THEN HE WAS GONE. JUST...GONE.
AS I START THE LONG WALK HOME, I REALIZE WHY HE DIDN'T FEEL LIKE TROUBLE.
I REALIZE THAT HE REMINDS ME OF MY UNCLE BEN.

BUT I'VE BEEN FOOLED BEFORE. AND USED BEFORE. ALSO MANIPULATED, STRUNG ALONG, TAKEN ADVANTAGE OF, MIND-MESSED AND UNWILLINGLY ADOPTED BY WACKOS LIKE OSBORN SR.
I DON'T TRUST ANYONE, ANYMORE.
I'D LIKE TO. LORD KNOWS I'D LIKE TO.
I JUST CAN'T. THAT'S ALL. I JUST...CAN'T. EVERY TIME I TRY...

...I END UP WAITING FOR THE OTHER SHOE TO DROP, FOR THE MONSTER TO COME OUT FROM BEHIND THE SMILING MASK.
AND AS MUCH AS I'D LOVE TO BE WRONG, IT'S ALMOST ALWAYS THERE, JUST WAITING TO PEEK OUT...
-- WHICH WILL COVER THE MONEY NEEDED TO DOCK YOUR BOAT, PLUS MAINTENANCE FEES, AND --

WE WON'T REQUIRE MAINTENANCE. JUST ACCESS TO THE PIER. WILL THIS COVER IT?
I...UMM...YES, YES, THAT SHOULD DO IT. BUT THERE'S STILL THE MATTER OF A CUSTOMS INSPECTION. YOU KNOW, MAKE SURE YOU'RE NOT BRINGING ANY ILLEGAL GOODS INTO THE COUNTRY.
OF COURSE, THEY CAN'T COME BY TO INSPECT YOUR VESSEL UNTIL THEY KNOW IT'S HERE... AND WE CAN EITHER SLOW DOWN THE PAPERWORK OR ACCELERATE IT...

YES, OF COURSE.
WILL *THIS* COVER IT?
THAT'LL DO JUST FINE. THANKS. THERE'S AN ABANDONED REPAIR HOUSING YOU CAN MOVE THE SHIP INTO, YOU KNOW, KEEP IT OUT OF THE WEATHER. AN OLD SHIP LIKE THAT, YOU GOTTA TAKE CARE OF IT.
YOU KNOW WHAT THEY SAY, OUT OF SIGHT, OUT OF MIND. HECK, I'LL FORGET ABOUT IT FOR AGES IF I DON'T SEE IT.
THANK YOU.

MY PLEASURE. GOOD DOING BUSINESS WITH YOU, MISTER...?
DEX. JUST... DEX.

...IS IT...IS IT DONE...?
YES, MORLUN. IT'S ALL SET. WE CAN MOVE TO COVER AS SOON AS THE WIND PICKS UP.
...GOOD... GOOD...

...TIME THEN... TO USE UP...THE LAST OF THE SUPPLIES...

...NO...NEIN, BITTE...I CAN... ICH KANNE...I HAVE NO MORE TO GIVE...PLEASE...ICH HABE... I HAVE NO MORE...
YES...YOU DO...NOW I MUST... TAKE IT. END THIS...AGONY... FOR YOU.

PLEEEAAAIIIIIII...

IT IS DONE.

IT IS OVER, DEX. DO NOT MOURN. REALLY, WHO EVER HEARD OF A GERMAN SUPER HERO, ANYWAY?
YOU KNOW WHERE WE ARE TO BE BERTHED?
YES.
THEN I WILL TAKE US THE REST OF THE WAY. IT WILL BE GOOD TO SEE THE LIGHTS OF THE CITY AGAIN AFTER SO LONG. THEN WE WILL GO INTO THE CITY, AND WE WILL EAT, AND DRINK.
THEN TOMORROW... TOMORROW, WE GO IN SEARCH OF HIS REPLACEMENT.
OR MENACE?
DAILY BUGLE

The Amazing Spider-Man #31
COVER ARTWORK

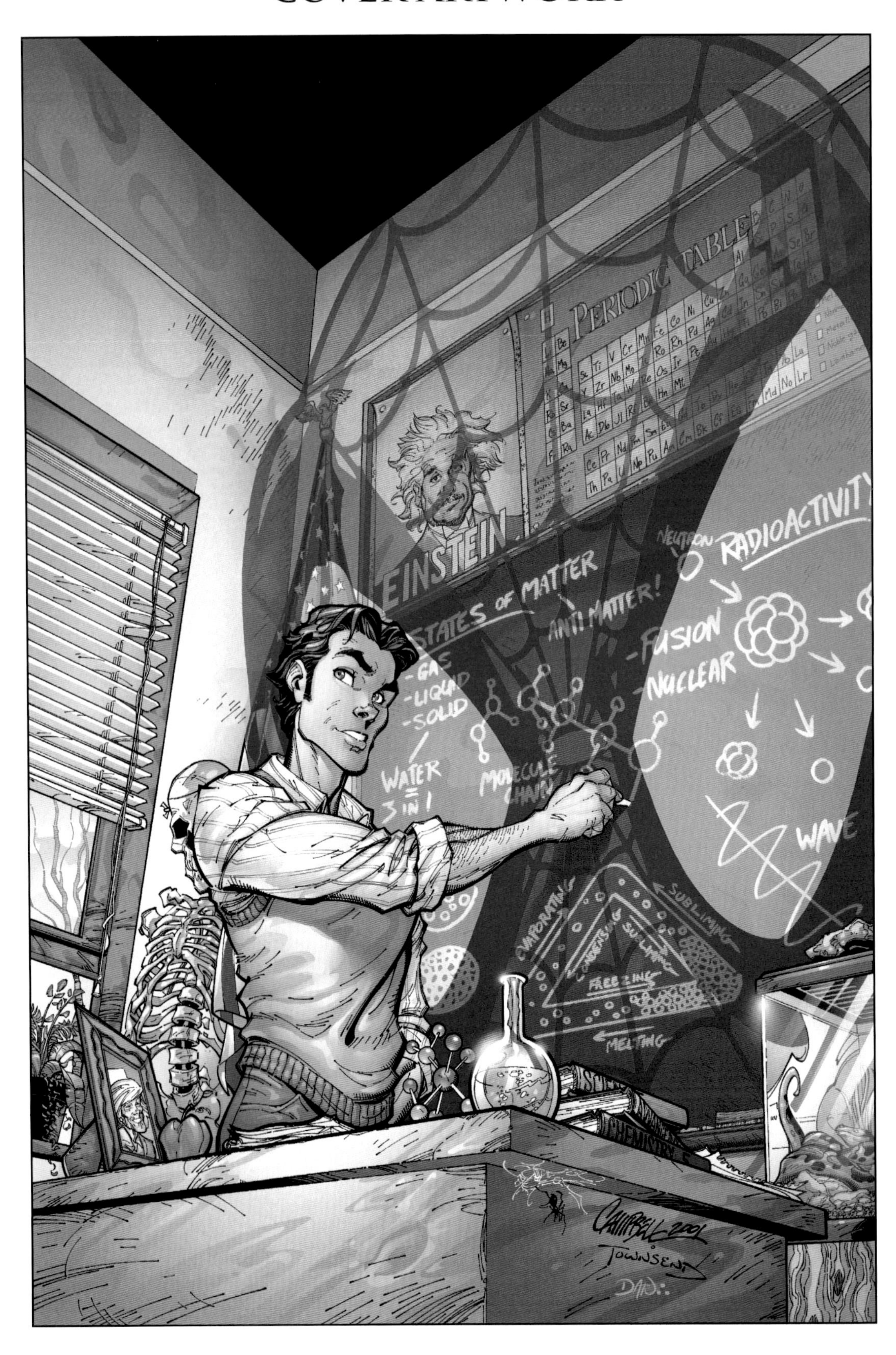

"I KNOW WHAT YOU'RE THINKING. AM I A FRIEND, OR AN ENEMY?
MY NAME IS EZEKIEL, AND I HAVE A QUESTION FOR YOU.
"THIS IS THE FIVE MILLION DOLLAR QUESTION. I'M ABOUT TO YANK YOUR CHAIN LIKE NOBODY ELSE EVER HAS BEFORE, AND NOBODY EVER WILL AGAIN. SO LISTEN CAREFULLY."
WOULD YOU LIKE ANOTHER EGG, PETER?
DID THE RADIATION ENABLE THE SPIDER TO GIVE YOU THESE POWERS?
"OR WAS THE SPIDER TRYING TO GIVE YOU THOSE POWERS BEFORE THE RADIATION KILLED IT?"
I SAID WOULD YOU LIKE ANOTHER EGG, PETER?

HMM? OH... UM...SORRY, AUNT MAY, I WAS --
-- A THOUSAND MILES AWAY, YES, I COULD TELL. I'VE SEEN THAT FARAWAY LOOK IN YOUR EYES SINCE YOU WERE THREE AND TRYING TO DECIDE WHETHER OR NOT CATS COULD FLY IF GIVEN SUFFICIENT INCENTIVE AND A HEAD START OFF THE ROOF.

WHEN THAT HAPPENS, I WAIT, AND REPEAT, JUST LIKE IT SAYS ON THOSE SHAMPOO BOTTLES, "WASH AND REPEAT," EXCEPT THERE'S NO WATER INVOLVED. EVENTUALLY, YOU COME BACK. YOU ALWAYS DO. IT'S JUST SOMETHING I'VE GOTTEN USED TO.
SO: PETER, LAST EGG. LAST EGG, PETER. WOULD YOU TWO LIKE TO GET TOGETHER?
YES, MA'AM.

SO ARE YOU GOING TO TELL ME WHAT'S GOT YOU SO DISTRACTED THIS MORNING? OR SHOULD I START CHECKING THE ROOF FOR MRS. BAILEY'S CAT?
IT'S...
HOW DO I EXPLAIN THAT LAST NIGHT SOMEONE I'VE NEVER MET BEFORE TURNED MY LIFE COMPLETELY UPSIDE DOWN?

SOMEBODY WITH POWERS VERY CLOSE TO MY OWN.
WHO SEEMS TO KNOW MORE ABOUT THE SOURCE OF MY POWER THAN I DO. AND WHO KNOWS MY REAL NAME.
TAKE CARE OF YOURSELF, P. I'LL BE IN TOUCH.
HOW DO YOU EXPLAIN? YOU DON'T. YOU JUST LIE. THE SAME WAY YOU'VE LIED FOR YEARS NOW. YOU LIE TO THE WOMAN WHO RAISED YOU AND MEANS MORE TO YOU THAN YOUR OWN LIFE.
IT SUCKS. I HATE IT. BUT IT'S NECESSARY.
...I WENT BY MY OLD HIGH SCHOOL THE OTHER DAY.
AH. NOSTALGIA. I SHOULD'VE RECOGNIZED THE LOOK. I SPEND QUITE A BIT OF TIME THERE MYSELF. HOW DID IT FEEL TO BE BACK?
WEIRD. IN SOME WAYS THAT SCHOOL WAS THE WORST PART OF MY LIFE. IN OTHERS, IT WAS THE BEST. BECAUSE THAT'S WHEN THINGS CHANGED FOR ME...
I MEAN, I CAUGHT SOME BREAKS, GOT BIT BY THE...SCIENCE BUG, STARTED SELLING MY PHOTOS TO THE BUGLE...THE SCHOOL WAS A REAL CHANCE FOR ME TO COME INTO MY OWN.
AND NOW...?
NOW... IT'S KIND OF FALLEN ON HARD TIMES. FRAYING AT THE EDGES, COVERED IN GRAFFITI...I GET THE FEELING THAT NOW IT'S AN EVEN TOUGHER PLACE FOR KIDS WHO ARE...WELL, LIKE I WAS AT THAT AGE.
BRIGHT? GIFTED?
ALONE.
PS 108

WELL, YOU KNOW, I WAS TALKING WITH MRS. CHAMPFER THE OTHER DAY.

I SAID I WAS TALKING WITH MRS. CHAMPFER THE OTHER DAY.
I WENT AWAY AGAIN, DIDN'T I?
YES.
OH.

HER SON, RONALD, WAS A SUBSTITUTE TEACHER THERE LAST YEAR. HE SAID IT'S HARD TO FIND GOOD TEACHERS WHO'LL WORK IN THAT DISTRICT. THE PAY ISN'T GREAT, AND THE NEIGHBORHOOD ISN'T WHAT IT USED TO BE.
HE SAID THEY'RE TRYING TO GET PROFESSIONALS IN A VARIETY OF FIELDS TO COME IN AND TEACH CLASS ONCE OR TWICE A WEEK. APPARENTLY, THEY CAN DEFER A TEACHING CREDENTIAL IN FAVOR OF WORK EXPERIENCE.

SO WHAT ARE YOU SUGGESTING?
NOT A THING.
YES, YOU ARE.
NO, I'M NOT. BUT IF I WERE --
AH-HA!

IF I WERE... I'D SUGGEST THAT MAYBE YOUR SENSE OF FAIRNESS IS TELLING YOU THAT THE KIDS THERE TODAY AREN'T GETTING THE SAME BREAKS YOU DID. AND MAYBE YOU COULD REPAY A LITTLE OF THAT, GIVE BACK TO THE SCHOOL THAT GAVE YOU SO MUCH.
IF I WERE OF A MIND TO SUGGEST SUCH THINGS.
WHICH, OF COURSE, I'M NOT.

I LOVE WATCHING THE GEARS BEGIN TO TURN...
"YOU SEEM RATHER DISTRACTED, SIR..."

HMM? OH, YES, I SUPPOSE I AM. I WAS OUT LATE LAST NIGHT. PLEASE, CONTINUE.
YES, SIR.
OVERSEAS HOLDINGS SHOW A TWELVE PERCENT INCREASE IN REVENUE OVER THIS SAME QUARTER LAST YEAR AND UP TEN PERCENT OVER THE COURSE OF THE LAST FISCAL YEAR...
AND HE WONDERS WHY I GET DISTRACTED...
SIR?
YOU'RE NEW HERE, AREN'T YOU?
I UHM... YES, SIR.
THEN LET ME MAKE IT SIMPLE FOR YOU. THIS IS A GENERAL MEETING FOR THE SAKE OF THE OTHER PARTNERS. SO ALL I WANT IS THE COFFEE TABLE FIGURE.
OF COURSE, SIR, I...UHM...THE WHAT?
THE COFFEE TABLE FIGURE.
IF I TOOK ALL THE MONEY WE HAVE, AND DUMPED IT OUT ONTO THE COFFEE TABLE OVER THERE, WHAT WOULD IT BE?
I'VE...NEVER BEEN ASKED THAT QUESTION BEFORE.
I RATHER GOT THAT IMPRESSION...
IF YOU CAN GIVE ME A MOMENT --
TAKE TWO.
YOU'RE ENJOYING THIS, AREN'T YOU?
IT'S A SMALL PLEASURE. AND SMALL PLEASURES ARE THE BEST PLEASURES. A WARM PAIR OF SLIPPERS, SAVING THE LAST CRISP PIECE OF BACON FOR YOUR LAST BITE IN THE MORNING, GIVING THE ACCOUNTANT A SNUGGIE --
I HAVE IT, SIR.
YES, PRINCE MISHKIN, WHAT'S YOUR PROGNOSIS?

ALLOWING FOR VARIATIONS IN REAL ASSETS VS. LIQUID ASSETS, AND TAKING INTO EFFECT THIS YEAR'S AMORTIZATION --
AHEM...
FIVE HUNDRED TWENTY-THREE MILLION, SEVEN HUNDRED FORTY THOUSAND DOLLARS... AND CHANGE.
THAT'S A VERY LARGE COFFEE TABLE, SIR.
IT'S A START.

NOW WE CAN GO OVER THE... UHM...

THAT IS...I CAN...SIR?

YES?
WHAT IS IT? I DON'T... SEE ANYTHING OUTSIDE.
NO, I DON'T EXPECT YOU WOULD.

YOU CAN GO NOW. THANK YOU FOR THE FIGURES.

YOU MADE CONTACT LAST NIGHT, DIDN'T YOU? AGAINST ALL OUR RECOMMENDATIONS --
I DID.
I JUST HOPE YOU KNOW WHAT YOU'RE DOING. YOU'RE NOT THE ONLY ONE AT RISK HERE.
IF THIS GOES BADLY, IT COULD DESTROY ALL OF US. RATHER THAN FACE THAT PROSPECT, GIVEN THE CHOICE...

"...I'D RATHER IT WAS HIM THAN US. HE IS EXPENDABLE."
"IS HE? I'M NOT SO SURE...

"NOT SO SURE AT ALL..."

YOU HAVEN'T EATEN YOUR CROISSANT.
I GUESS I'M NOT AS HUNGRY AS I THOUGHT.
YOU SHOULD EAT. KEEP YOUR STRENGTH UP. I DO. BUT I'VE HAD LONGER THAN YOU TO ACQUIRE GOOD HABITS.
MUCH LONGER.
EAT YOUR CROISSANT, DEX.
YES, MORLUN.

DO YOU KNOW WHY HUMANS ARE A PEOPLE OF HOPE? BECAUSE YOU MAKE THINGS LIKE CROISSANTS AND PASTRY. PASTRY IN PARTICULAR. YOU MAKE SOMETHING OF ASTONISHING BEAUTY, CAREFULLY DECORATED, FRAGILE, LOVELY, KNOWING THAT THE PERSON WHO RECEIVES IT WILL APPRECIATE THAT BEAUTY FOR ONLY FOR ABOUT TWO SECONDS BEFORE DEVOURING IT.
IN THAT, WE HAVE SOMETHING IN COMMON.

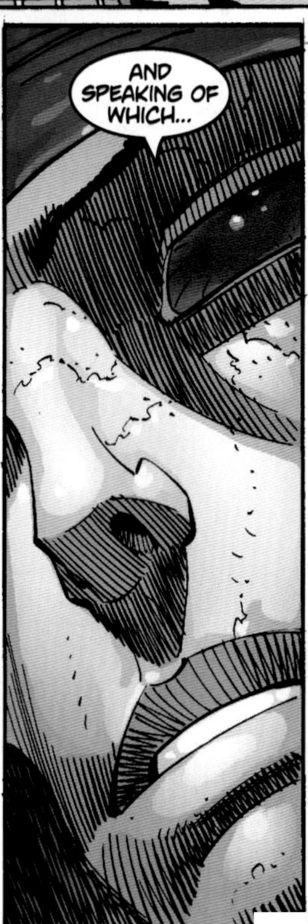

AND SPEAKING OF WHICH...

OHJEEZ --!
WHAT THE HECK WAS THAT? SPIDER-SENSE WENT NUTS, LIKE NOTHING I'VE EVER FELT BEFORE.
LIKE THE WORD *HIDE* WAS BURNED ACROSS MY BRAIN IN LETTERS TEN FEET HIGH.

DON'T SEE ANYTHING...SO WHY THE SPIDEY-SENSE BULLET THROUGH THE BRAIN?
THIS IS RIDICULOUS. I HAVE TO GET GOING. I CAN'T JUST HIDE HERE UNDER A LEDGE ALL DAY.
SIRICOS
I'LL JUST... SHOOT A WEB AND LEAP OUT THERE AND GET GOING ON MY WAY. I'LL JUST...
...SLIP AROUND THIS WAY.
CAREFULLY DECORATED. FRAGILE. LOVELY. DOOMED.
SAD, REALLY. BUT THEN IT'S ALWAYS SAD. ALWAYS HAS BEEN, ALWAYS WILL BE. IT'S YOUR LOT, YOU KNOW, TO BE THINGS OF BEAUTY, HERE FOR A MOMENT, A FLICKER, AND GONE. SO SAD...
HOW WAS THE CROISSANT?
FINE.
GOOD.
KILL ME.
NOT TODAY.
SOON, THOUGH?
WE'LL SEE...
...NOW DRINK YOUR COFFEE. IT'S AN ORANGE MOCHA.
BEFORE IT GET'S COLD.
"ICK! SPIDER! GET IT!"

I HATE SPIDERS. I SWEAR THEY THEY JUST KNOW WHEN YOU'RE ABOUT TO SMUSH 'EM AND THEY SCURRY UNDER A LEDGE OR A DOOR AND YOU CAN'T GET TO THEM AND I HATE SPIDERS --
YOU MENTIONED THAT PART ALREADY.
EXIT

HATE HATE HATE HATE HATE HATE!

CONCEDING DEFEAT, GENERAL?
FOR NOW. SOONER OR LATER, I'LL NAIL HIM.
YOU ASK ME, IF EVERY ICKY SPIDER-THINGIE ON THE PLANET WAS FRIED DEAD ON THE SPOT, IT'D BE A BETTER WORLD FOR EVERYBODY.

YES...?
UHM...I'M PETER PARKER...I CALLED ABOUT THE WORK EXPERIENCE TEACHING CREDENTIAL...
RIGHT... RIGHT...

I'LL JUST GET THE PAPERWORK.
STUPID SPIDER...

WHAT THE --

...GUN...
GUN!
CRACK
CRACK CRACK
DOWN!
CRACK
CRACK
CRACK
I MOVE MYSELF WITHOUT THINKING, PUTTING MYSELF BETWEEN THEM AND THE BULLETS.
I HAVE TO MOVE SLOWER THAN USUAL TO AVOID HURTING THEM, BUT I DON'T CARE ABOUT THE ADDED RISK. I DON'T EVEN CARE ABOUT WHAT ANYONE MIGHT THINK IF THEY SEE ME.
THERE'S A TIME FOR SECRET IDENTITIES AND THERE'S A TIME TO SAVE LIVES AND BY GOD HE'S NOT GOING TO HURT THESE KIDS AND I DON'T CARE IF I GET KILLED DOING IT, HE'S NOT GOING TO GET TO THEM.
HE'S NOT.
HE'S NOT.

GOT YOU!

THEY'RE SCARED. THEY THINK THEY'RE GOING TO DIE.

IT'S NOT RIGHT. KIDS SHOULDN'T HAVE TO COME TO SCHOOL THINKING THEY'RE GOING TO DIE.

I WON'T HAVE IT.

I...I DON'T HEAR ANY MORE SHOTS. MAYBE...MAYBE HE'S STOPPED. MAYBE HE'S GONE AWAY.

NO. HE'S INSIDE.

WHAT... WHAT'RE WE GONNA DO?
SHUT UP! YOU WANNA LET HIM KNOW WE'RE HERE, STUPID? BESIDES, YOU CAN'T DO SQUAT, YOU CREEP, SO YOU MAY AS WELL JUST SHUT UP.
ADVANCED CHEMISTRY

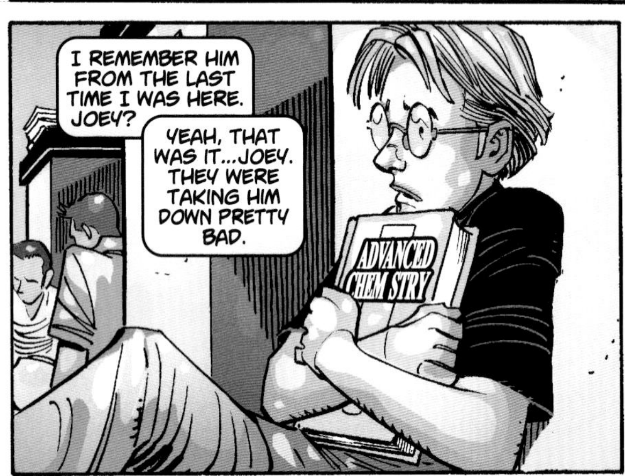
I REMEMBER HIM FROM THE LAST TIME I WAS HERE. JOEY?
YEAH, THAT WAS IT...JOEY. THEY WERE TAKING HIM DOWN PRETTY BAD.
ADVANCED CHEM STRY

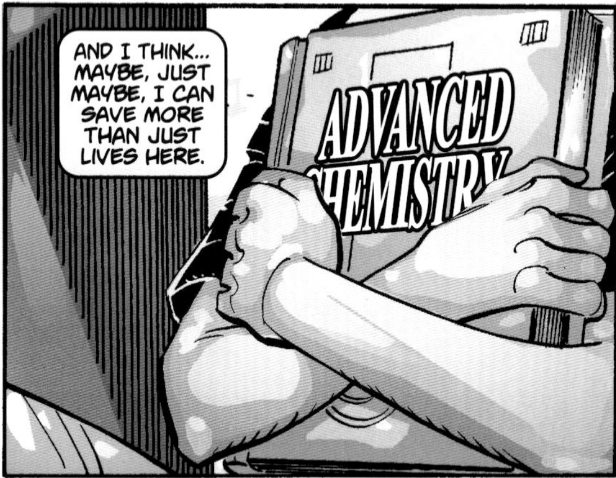
AND I THINK... MAYBE, JUST MAYBE, I CAN SAVE MORE THAN JUST LIVES HERE.
ADVANCED

YOU'RE JOEY, RIGHT?
UH-HUH...
YOU PRETTY GOOD AT CHEMISTRY?
UH-HUH...
WHAT'RE YOU --

I'M NOT TALKING TO YOU.
LISTEN TO ME CLOSELY, JOEY... I DON'T KNOW IF HE'S RELOADING OR LOOKING FOR SOME TARGET IN PARTICULAR, BUT EITHER WAY WE DON'T HAVE MUCH TIME.
LOOK BEHIND YOU.
ADVANCED

I'M THINKING HE CAN'T HIT WHAT HE CAN'T SEE. WHAT DO YOU THINK?

I'M GOING BACK OUT THERE, AND I COULD REALLY USE THE HELP. OKAY?
O-OKAY. BUT WHAT IF HE SEES ME?
HE WON'T. I SWEAR IT.

READY?
YEAH... I THINK SO...
ON THREE.
WHAT'RE YOU --
ONE... TWO...

THREE!

I CAN FIND THE SHOOTER. BUT I DON'T WANT HIM DOING ANY MORE HARM BEFORE I CAN GET MY HANDS ON HIM.
C'MON, JOEY, DON'T LET ME DOWN.
JOEY CASTONE! GET DOWN FROM THERE RIGHT NOW! I SAID GET DOWN--
-- TANNIC ACID, WHERE'S THE TANNIC ACID --
I'LL HAVE YOU ON REPORT, YOUNG MAN!
GOT IT!
WHAT'S THAT... FIRE?
NO...THERE'S NO SMELL OF BURNING, STAY DOWN!
WAY TO GO, JOEY...WAY TO GO.

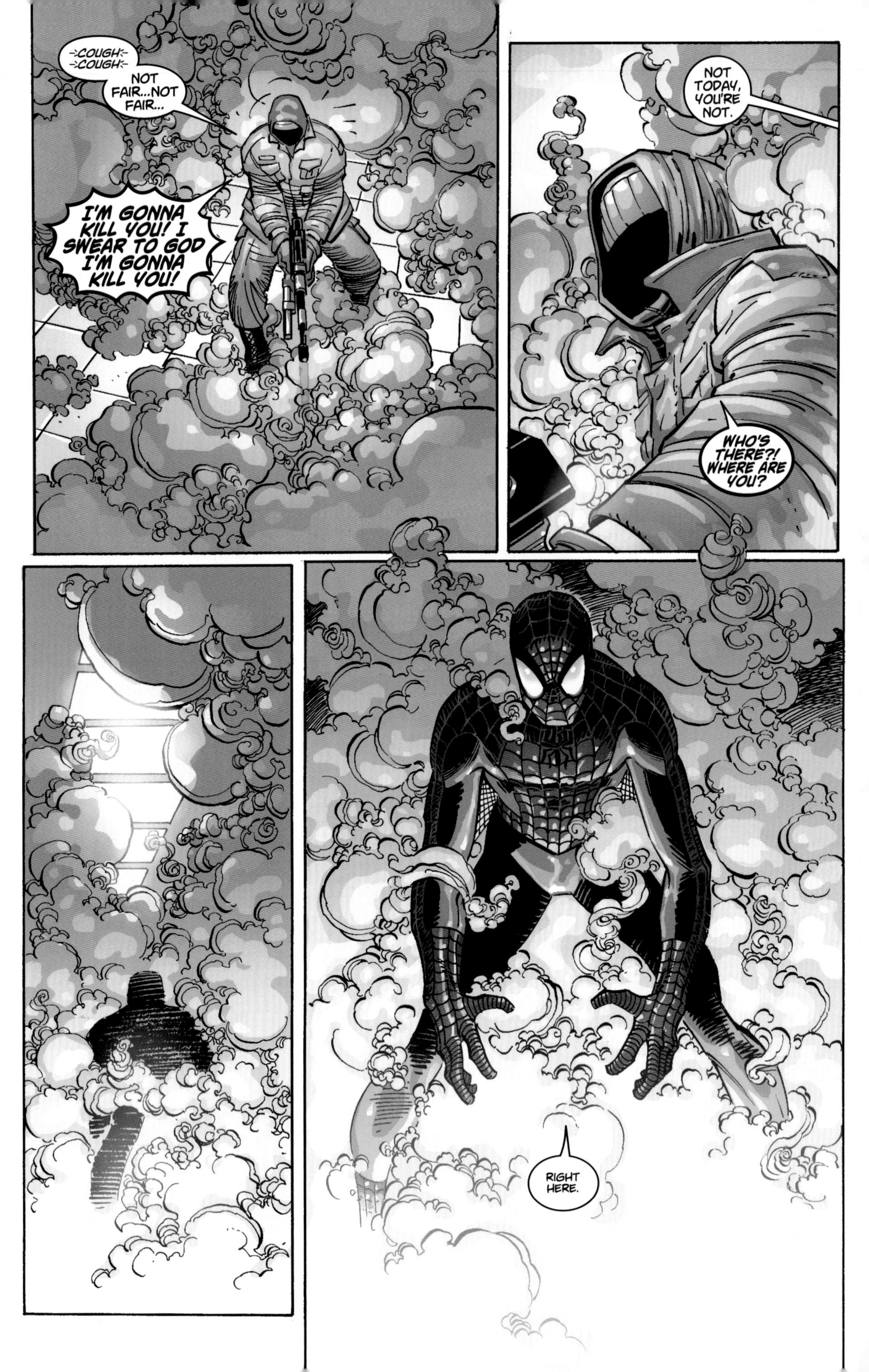

COUGH
COUGH
NOT FAIR...NOT FAIR...
I'M GONNA KILL YOU! I SWEAR TO GOD I'M GONNA KILL YOU!
NOT TODAY, YOU'RE NOT.
WHO'S THERE?! WHERE ARE YOU?
RIGHT HERE.

YAAAAGGHHH!

GET UP! WHO ARE YOU? WHAT'S WRONG WITH --

...OH MY GOD...

IT'S NOT FAIR...IT'S NOT FAIR...THEY KEEP BEATING ME UP ALL THE TIME...I CAN'T TAKE IT ANYMORE... I CAN'T TAKE IT ANYMORE...

I JUST CAN'T TAKE IT ANYMORE...
THE KID JUST SNAPPED.

I HAD HIM IN ONE OF MY CLASSES. A REAL SMART KID. AN "A" STUDENT. THEY SAID HE WAS A PRODIGY OR SOMETHING.
THE OTHER KIDS WERE PRETTY BRUTAL TO HIM. PICKED ON HIM FOR ALL THREE YEARS. BUT, Y'KNOW, YOU HAVE TO STAND UP ON YOUR OWN SOMETIMES.

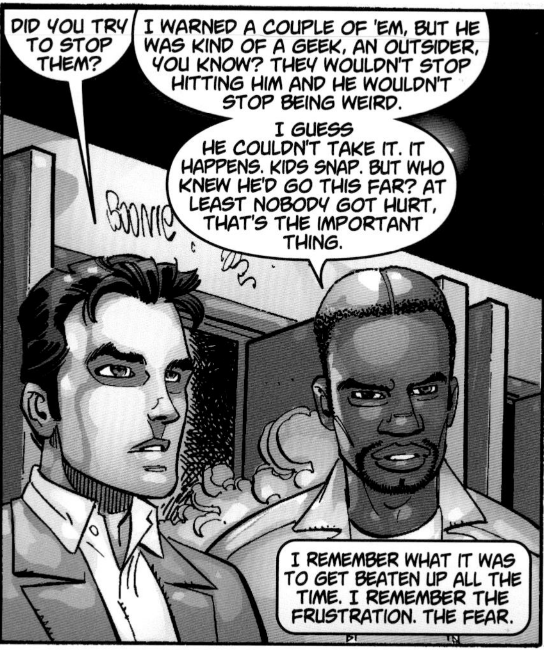
DID YOU TRY TO STOP THEM?
I WARNED A COUPLE OF 'EM, BUT HE WAS KIND OF A GEEK, AN OUTSIDER, YOU KNOW? THEY WOULDN'T STOP HITTING HIM AND HE WOULDN'T STOP BEING WEIRD.
I GUESS HE COULDN'T TAKE IT. IT HAPPENS. KIDS SNAP. BUT WHO KNEW HE'D GO THIS FAR? AT LEAST NOBODY GOT HURT, THAT'S THE IMPORTANT THING.
BOONIE
I REMEMBER WHAT IT WAS TO GET BEATEN UP ALL THE TIME. I REMEMBER THE FRUSTRATION. THE FEAR.

THE RAGE. THE MINDLESS RAGE THAT MAKES YOU FEEL YOU'D DO ANYTHING TO GET BACK AT THE ONES WHO BRING YOU PAIN FOR NO OTHER REASON THAN THEY THINK IT'S FUN.
THAT COULD HAVE BEEN ME. THAT COULD BE JOEY SOMEDAY.
POLI

I HEAR YOU HELPED SAVE SOME OF THE KIDS. GOOD FOR YOU.
AND YOU?
I WAS BACK BY THE RACQUETBALL COURT. FIGURED THE BEST THING I COULD DO WAS TO KEEP MY HEAD DOWN AND LET THE RIGHT PEOPLE DO THEIR JOB.

YEAH, WELL... THEY DID. THEY DID THAT INDEED.
I QUIT... THAT'S IT, I'VE HAD IT, THIS PLACE IS A FREAKIN' JUNGLE, I'M OUTTA HERE!

I DON'T BLAME HIM. SCIENCE IS WASTED ON MOST OF THESE KIDS ANYWAY. A LOT OF 'EM ARE GOING NOWHERE FAST.
YEP. HE'S NOT THE FIRST ONE TO GET OUT OF HERE. WON'T BE THE LAST, EITHER.
WE ALL HAVE TO FACE THE TRUTH. YOU DO WHAT YOU CAN. BUT YOU CAN'T SAVE ALL OF THEM.
PHYS ED DEPT

SO, ANYWAY, I DIDN'T GET YOUR NAME.
WHO AM I?

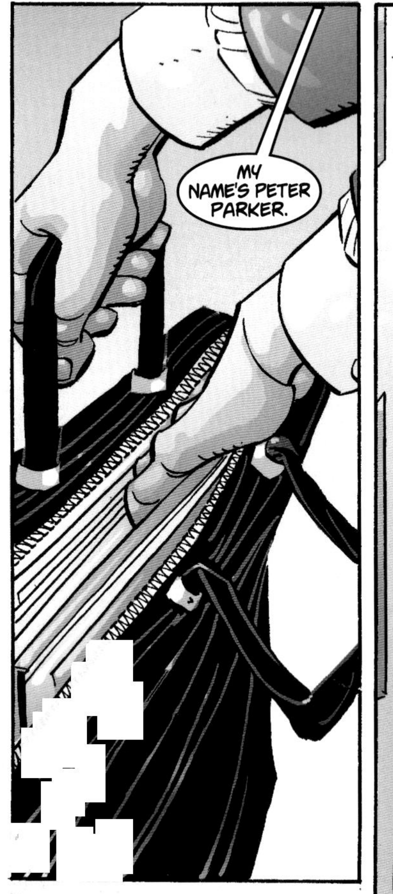
MY NAME'S PETER PARKER.

I'M THE NEW SCIENCE TEACHER.
PARKER, P.
RESUME

The Amazing Spider-Man #32
Cover Artwork

-- UNIT 472, WE CONFIRM THAT THE SUSPECT HAS TAKEN A HOSTAGE, REPEAT, THE SUSPECT HAS TAKEN A HOSTAGE --
GET BACK OR I'LL KILL HER! I SWEAR TO GOD I'LL KILL HER!
DO AS HE SAYS, PULL BACK, GIVE HIM SOME ROOM! WE DON'T WANT HIM SHOOTING THE HOSTAGE!

NOT STOPPIN'...NO WAY, WE'RE NOT STOPPIN' TILL WE HIT THE STATE LINE, THEY'RE NOT TAKING ME ALIVE... I DIE, YOU DIE...
PLEASE, I --
SHUTTUP!

AIN'T NOBODY STOPPING US NOW!
RTS
SIRICO

WHUMP
WHAT THE HELL --

--EEEEEEKKK!
AAAAAGGHH!

YAAAGGGHH!
EEEEEEKKK!

HUNH! HUNH! HUNH!
SO...

...CAN I, LIKE, DROP YOU SOMEWHERE?

FUNNY HOW I ALWAYS HAVE THAT EFFECT ON WOMEN... CAN'T FIGURE IT OUT...

FREAK... DAMN FREAK... NOT GONNA GET ME, NOT GONNA --
PSSST... HEY, EINSTEIN --
-- UP HERE!
YIPE!
SEE, THING IS, I'D LOVE TO HANG OUT AND CONTINUE THIS FASCINATING DIALOGUE --
LEMME GOLEMMEGO LEMMEGO!
EXACTLY. YOU BIG OL' SMART GUYS WITH YOUR BIG CITY WAYS AND YOUR FANCY TALK. BUT I'M ALMOST LATE FOR WORK.
SO THIS IS GOING TO BE...QUICK.
WHICH WOULD YOU PREFER: TO BE UNCONSCIOUS OR INSULTED?
PICK ONE.
I... I --
GOOD CHOICE.
FOUR-DAVID-NINE, WE ARE IN PURSUIT! WE ARE --
HOLY --!

WHAT THE #$%@ ARE YOU LOOKIN' AT?
LOSER
"HUMANS ARE FUNNY CREATURES...

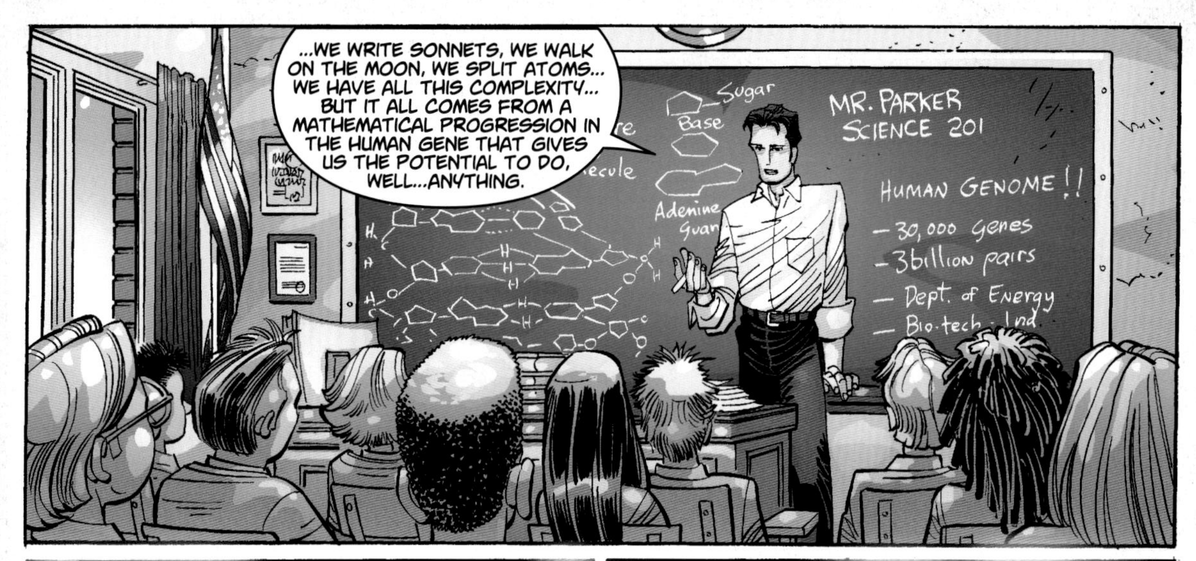
...WE WRITE SONNETS, WE WALK ON THE MOON, WE SPLIT ATOMS... WE HAVE ALL THIS COMPLEXITY... BUT IT ALL COMES FROM A MATHEMATICAL PROGRESSION IN THE HUMAN GENE THAT GIVES US THE POTENTIAL TO DO, WELL...ANYTHING.
Sugar
Base
Adenine
MR. PARKER
SCIENCE 201
HUMAN GENOME!!
— 30,000 Genes
— 3billion pairs
— Dept. of Energy
— Bio-tech. Ind.

THAT'S WHAT SO MANY DON'T UNDERSTAND. MUSIC IS MATH. ART IS MATH. WE...ARE MATH. THE MATH IN OUR GENES FUNNELS INTO THE MATH OF OUR DREAMS, OUR ART, OUR AMBITION.
SCIENCE ISN'T JUST BEAKERS AND TEST TUBES...IT'S WHO AND WHAT WE ARE. ARTISTIC. ECCENTRIC. HUMAN.
I WATCH THEM, AND I SEE THE LIGHT GO ON IN A FEW EYES. JUST A VERY FEW EYES.

WHEN I WAS THEIR AGE, I WAS A KID. NOW, TODAY, THEY'RE THE SAME AGE... BUT THEY'RE NOT KIDS ANYMORE. SO MUCH OF THEIR INNOCENCE IS GONE. THE SENSE OF WONDER IS GONE. THEIR ROAD IS HARDER.

SO I'LL JUST WORK THAT MUCH HARDER TO GET THROUGH. I KNOW I CAN DO IT. I HAVE TO DO IT.
SOMEHOW.
-- SO THE FUNNY THING IS... AND YOU'RE GONNA LOVE THIS...IT ALL STARTED WITH SCIENTISTS MESSING AROUND WITH THE LOVE LIVES OF FRUIT FLIES...
RRIINNNNNGG

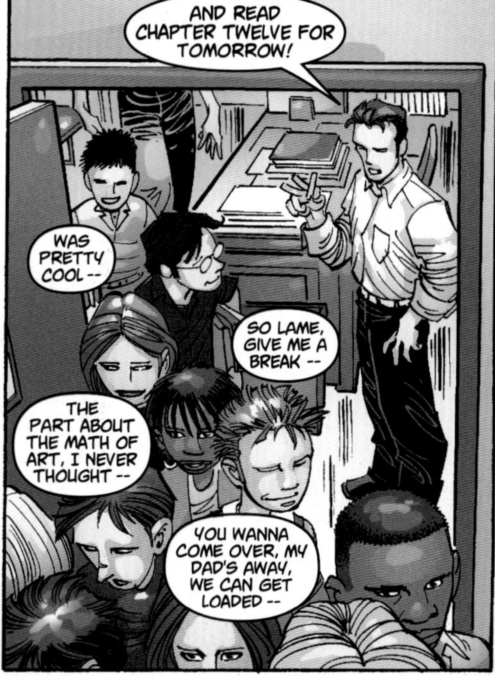
AND READ CHAPTER TWELVE FOR TOMORROW!
WAS PRETTY COOL --
SO LAME, GIVE ME A BREAK --
THE PART ABOUT THE MATH OF ART, I NEVER THOUGHT --
YOU WANNA COME OVER, MY DAD'S AWAY, WE CAN GET LOADED --

PETER, GOOD, THERE YOU ARE.
PRINCIPAL HARRINGTON, HI, WHAT'S --
CAN I SEE YOU IN MY OFFICE FOR A MOMENT?
SWELL. I'M BACK IN MY OLD HIGH SCHOOL FOR ONE DAY AND ALREADY I'M BEING SENT TO THE PRINCIPAL'S OFFICE.
HOW'S YOUR FIRST DAY GOING?
FINE...FINE... LISTEN, IS THERE ANYTHING WRONG, OR --
GOOD, GOOD. YOU KNOW, WHEN YOU APPLIED FOR WORK HERE, WE HAD NO IDEA YOU HAD SUCH... WELL, GENEROUS FRIENDS.

I HAVE GENEROUS FRIENDS?
I HAVE FRIENDS?
HA! VERY FUNNY. YOU KNOW, I WAS AWARE THAT YOU WERE GOOD AT WHAT YOU DO, BUT I DIDN'T KNOW YOU WERE ACTUALLY FUNNY.
YEAH, I GET THAT A LOT.

HERE WE GO, WE CAN JUST --
YOU --!
HI, P. --

-- HOW'S IT GOING?
EZEKIEL... WHAT'RE YOU DOING --
OH, GOOD, THEN IT IS A SURPRISE.
WHAT'S A SURPRISE?

YOUR FRIEND HAS JUST DONATED $100,000 TO PURCHASE NEW SCIENCE EQUIPMENT FOR THE SCHOOL.
I WOULD'VE DONATED A PARTICLE ACCELERATOR BUT I COULDN'T FIT IT IN THE BACK OF THE CAR.
ISN'T THAT WONDERFUL?

YEAH. WONDERFUL.
SO HOW ABOUT YOU AND ME STEP OUTSIDE AND TALK ABOUT JUST HOW WONDERFUL YOU ARE TO TRACK ME DOWN LIKE THIS.
LOVE TO. I KNOW JUST THE PLACE.

THAT'S THE THING ABOUT NEW YORK, P. YOU GET THE BEST PIZZA HERE. I THINK IT HAS SOMETHING TO DO WITH THE QUALITY OF THE MOZZARELLA --
WHY ARE YOU DOING THIS?
BECAUSE I LIKE PIZZA.
THAT'S NOT WHAT I'M TALKING ABOUT.

YOU KNOW WHO AND WHAT I AM. YOU'VE CLEARLY BEEN KEEPING TABS ON ME, SINCE YOU KNOW ABOUT MY NEW JOB.
THAT'S CORRECT. I FIGURE YOU TOOK ON THE JOB TO DO SOME GOOD. I THINK IT'S A GREAT IDEA. FIGURED I'D DO THE SAME. IT'S LAUDABLE, IT'S DEDUCTIBLE...
...AND IT GOT YOUR ATTENTION.
LOOK, PETER, I KNOW YOU DON'T HAVE ANY REASON TO TRUST ME. AND I'M NOT SAYING YOU SHOULD.

ALL I'M SAYING IS THAT YOU'RE IN DANGER, AND THE INFORMATION I HAVE MAY HELP YOU SURVIVE IT.
AND WHAT'S THAT TO YOU?
WE'RE... KINDRED SPIRITS, REMEMBER? I KNOW THINGS ABOUT YOUR POWERS EVEN YOU DON'T KNOW. SO MAYBE YOU SHOULD AT LEAST HEAR ME OUT.

FINE. YOU WANT TO TALK? GO RIGHT AHEAD.
AND IT'S THE WATER THAT GOES INTO THE DOUGH, NOT THE MOZZARELLA, EVERYBODY KNOWS THAT...
SO WHAT DO YOU THINK YOU KNOW ABOUT MY POWERS THAT I DON'T? I MEAN, WHAT, CAN I TALK TO SPIDERS OR SOMETHING?

HOW DO YOU KNOW YOU CAN'T? HAVE YOU EVER TRIED?
NO.
SO GIVE IT A SHOT.
YOU'RE KIDDING.
IS THIS THE FACE OF A KIDDER? GO ON.

SO...HOW'S IT GOING? EAT ANY GOOD FLIES TODAY?

NOTHING.
OF COURSE NOT. BECAUSE INDIVIDUALLY, SPIDERS ARE MORONS.
THEN WHY --
I SAID *INDIVIDUALLY* SPIDERS ARE MORONS. BUT COLLECTIVELY, THEY FORM ONE, SINGULAR THOUGHT.
AND WHAT'S THAT?
WELL...THAT'S THE MYSTERY, ISN'T IT?
ASK A STUPID QUESTION YOU GET A STUPID ANSWER...
NO, PETER. IT'S NOT STUPID AT ALL.
YOU ASKED ME TO TELL YOU WHAT I KNOW ABOUT YOUR POWER THAT YOU DON'T. BUT IT'S NOT AS SIMPLE AS TELLING YOU WHERE THE RIGHT BUTTON IS ON THE DASHBOARD OF A NEW CAR. YOU HAVE TO RECONSIDER HOW YOU'VE LOOKED AT YOUR LIFE.
WHO AND WHAT YOU ARE BRIDGES THE GAP BETWEEN SPIDER AND MAN. BUT YOU'RE NOT THE FIRST. THERE ARE TOTEMISTIC POWERS THAT GO BACK TO THE DAWN OF TIME. THEIR PRESENCE REMAINS WITH US ALMOST LIKE A RACE MEMORY.

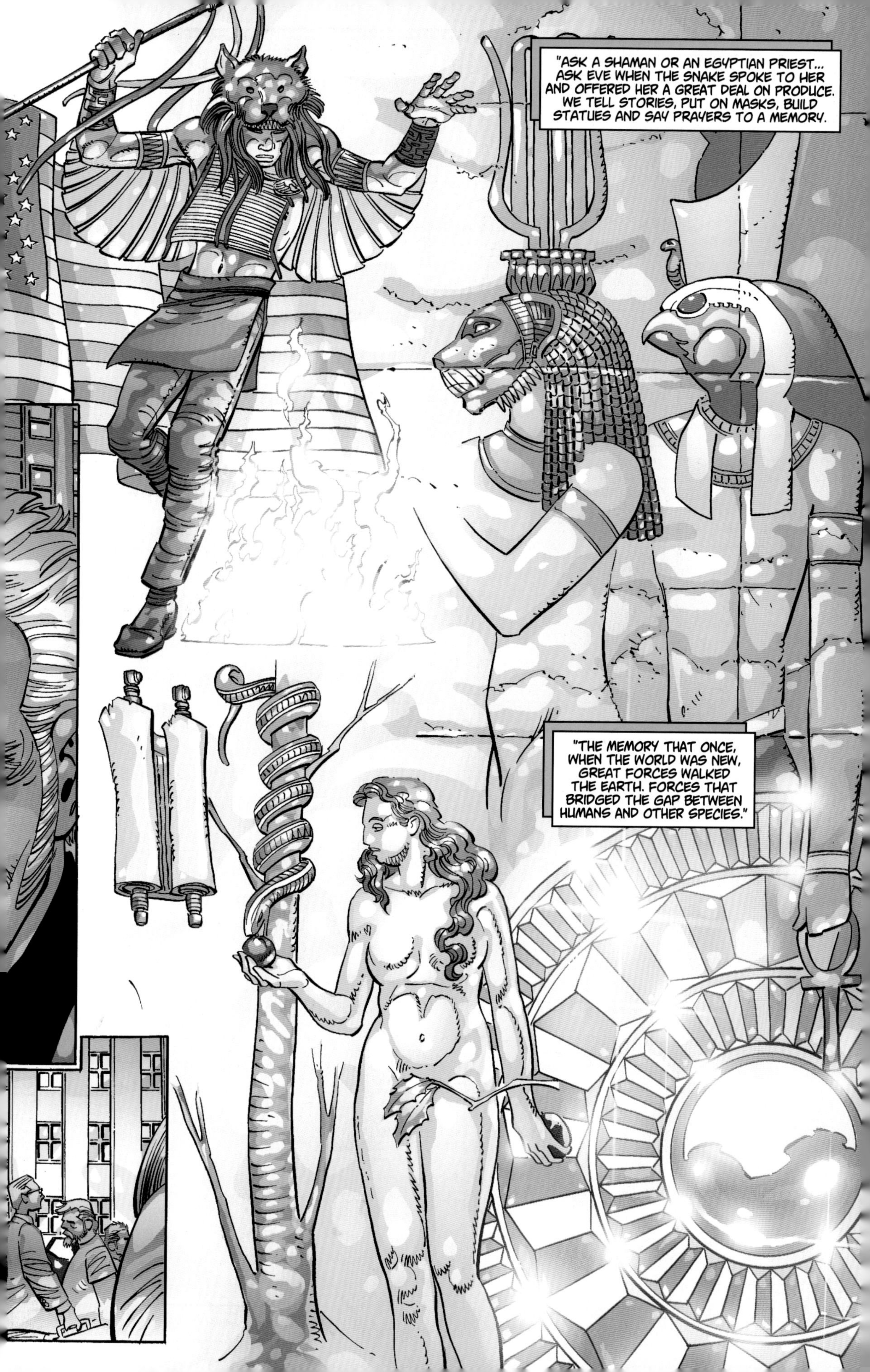
"ASK A SHAMAN OR AN EGYPTIAN PRIEST... ASK EVE WHEN THE SNAKE SPOKE TO HER AND OFFERED HER A GREAT DEAL ON PRODUCE. WE TELL STORIES, PUT ON MASKS, BUILD STATUES AND SAY PRAYERS TO A MEMORY.
"THE MEMORY THAT ONCE, WHEN THE WORLD WAS NEW, GREAT FORCES WALKED THE EARTH. FORCES THAT BRIDGED THE GAP BETWEEN HUMANS AND OTHER SPECIES."

WE DO THESE THINGS OUT OF AN ALMOST CELLULAR NEED TO RECREATE THAT TRUTH, TO GET A MOMENTARY TASTE OF TOTEMISTIC FORCE. SOME DO IT FOR RITUAL. OTHERS FOR A GREATER UNDERSTANDING OF THE WORLD AROUND THEM.
AND SOME DO IT TO PROJECT A SENSE OF POWER.
AND YOU SHOULD KNOW, PETER. YOU'VE FOUGHT MANY OF THEM.
LOOK, EZEKIEL, YOU MAY OR MAY NOT BE RIGHT ABOUT SOME OF THIS, BUT I KNOW WHO I'VE FOUGHT, AND NONE OF THEM ARE --
YOU'RE STILL NOT LISTENING.
YOU EVER HEAR THE PHRASE "YOU KNOW A MAN BY HIS ENEMIES"? LOOK AROUND...
"CAPTAIN AMERICA WOUND UP WITH GUYS LIKE BARON ZEMO AND THE RED SKULL.
"THE X-MEN GOT MAGNETO.
"THOR'S GOT LOKI...

ONE TYPE ATTRACTS ANOTHER, SIMILAR TYPE. GODS AGAINST GODS, PATRIOTS AGAINST PEOPLE WHO THINK THEY'RE PATRIOTS, MUTANTS AGAINST MUTANTS. THE KIND OF ENEMY YOU GET TELLS SOMEONE A LOT ABOUT THE KIND OF PERSON YOU ARE.
NOW CONSIDER YOUR SITUATION. FROM THE VERY BEGINNING, MORE THAN ANYONE ELSE OUT THERE, YOU HAVE BEEN BESET BY TOTEMISTIC PRETENDERS. AND THE KICKER IS...THEY PROBABLY DON'T EVEN REALIZE WHAT THEY'RE DOING.
"VULTURES AND CROCODILES, SCORPIONS AND COBRAS, JACKALS AND CATS AND FOXES AND OCTOPI AND EVERYTHING IN BETWEEN. LOOK AT THEM, PETER. LOOK AT THE PATTERN.
"THESE PEOPLE HAVE BEEN GUIDED BY URGES AND EVENTS OUTSIDE THEIR CONTROL, BEYOND EVEN THEIR UNDERSTANDING... BUT WHICH HAVE LED THEM TO EMBRACE A TOTEM, TO TRY AND GRAFT THE POWER OF THAT IMAGE ONTO THEIR OWN SOULS, THEIR OWN BODIES.
"OVER THE YEARS YOU FOUGHT THEM, AND STROVE WITH THEM, BUT YOU NEVER SAW THEM FOR WHAT THEY ARE.
"PRETENDERS."

"BUT IF THEY'RE PRETENDERS... THEN WHAT DOES THAT MAKE ME?"
"THE REAL DEAL, PETER.
"THE REAL DEAL..."
I SEE...
NO, YOU DON'T. NOT REALLY, AND NOT YET. BUT YOU WILL.
SO IF I'M THE REAL DEAL, WHERE DO YOU FIT INTO ALL OF THIS? HOW DID YOU GET YOUR... ABILITIES?
ME?
"MY ROAD... WAS NOT QUITE THE SAME AS YOURS."

"IT WAS NOT AS...PURE AS YOURS.

"I'LL TELL YOU ABOUT IT SOMETIME.

"I'M SURE YOU'LL GET A KICK OUT OF IT."

PRETENDERS ALWAYS HATE THE REAL DEAL. THEY MAY NOT EVEN RECOGNIZE THE IMPULSE FOR WHAT IT IS, BUT IT DRIVES THEM TO AN ALMOST PATHOLOGICAL HATRED TO DESTROY THAT WHICH THEY CAN NEVER BE.
AND IN THAT RESPECT, AS HUNTERS, THEY ARE STILL ONLY PRETENDERS. STILL ONLY ECHOES OF SOMETHING FAR DARKER...AND INFINITELY MORE LETHAL.

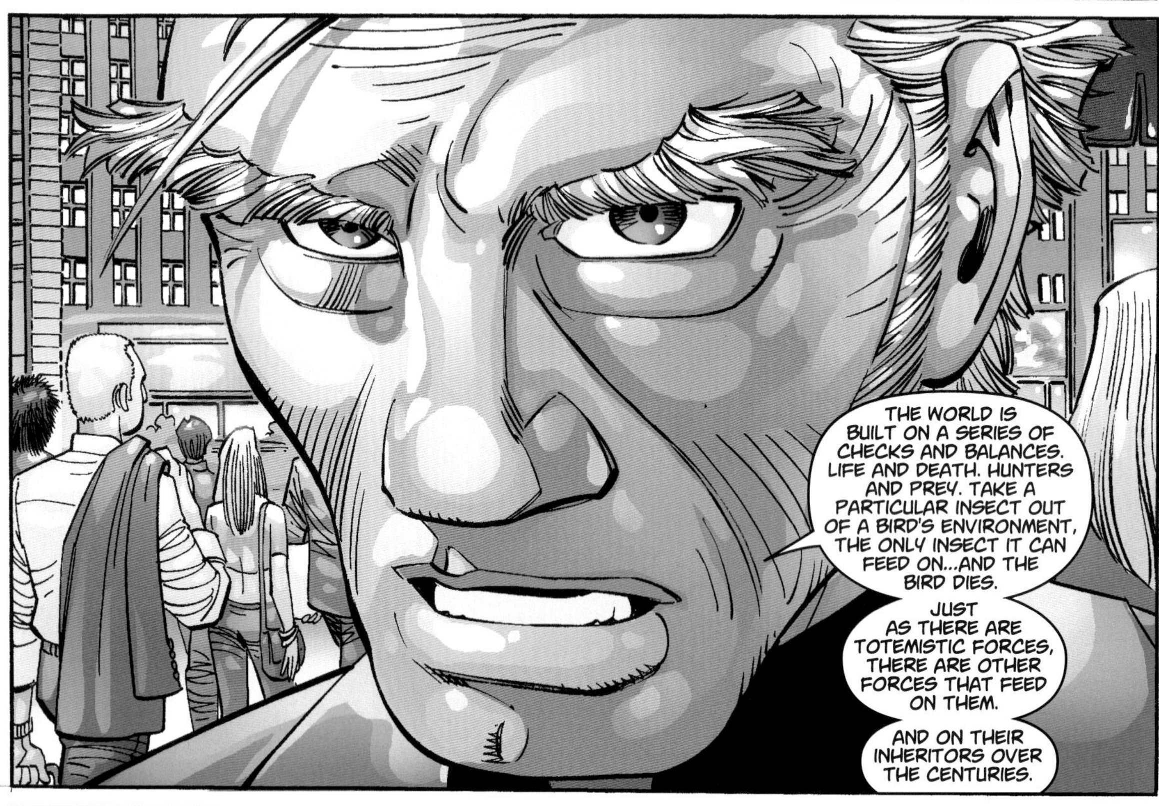
THE WORLD IS BUILT ON A SERIES OF CHECKS AND BALANCES. LIFE AND DEATH. HUNTERS AND PREY. TAKE A PARTICULAR INSECT OUT OF A BIRD'S ENVIRONMENT, THE ONLY INSECT IT CAN FEED ON...AND THE BIRD DIES.
JUST AS THERE ARE TOTEMISTIC FORCES, THERE ARE OTHER FORCES THAT FEED ON THEM.
AND ON THEIR INHERITORS OVER THE CENTURIES.

ON PEOPLE... LIKE YOU.

"ONLY A FEW OF THEM STILL WALK THE EARTH. THEY ARE USED TO HUNTING DOWN YOUR KIND. THEY HAVE DONE SO FOR UNCOUNTED CENTURIES. THEY CAN SUSTAIN THEMSELVES ON LESSER SOURCES FOR A WHILE, BUT EVERY SO OFTEN, THEY MUST GO BACK TO THE SOURCE, MUST DRINK DEEP, MUST FEED COMPLETELY."
"AND YOU'RE SAYING THAT ONE OF THEM HAS COME HERE? LOOKING FOR ME?"
"YES.

"YOU...AND TO A LESSER EXTENT, I...CAN SENSE HIS PRESENCE ON AN ALMOST CELLULAR LEVEL. I KNOW YOU'VE FELT HIM, FELT SOMETHING WRONG."
"SO WHY HASN'T HE COME AFTER ME?"
HMMM... I DON'T KNOW...

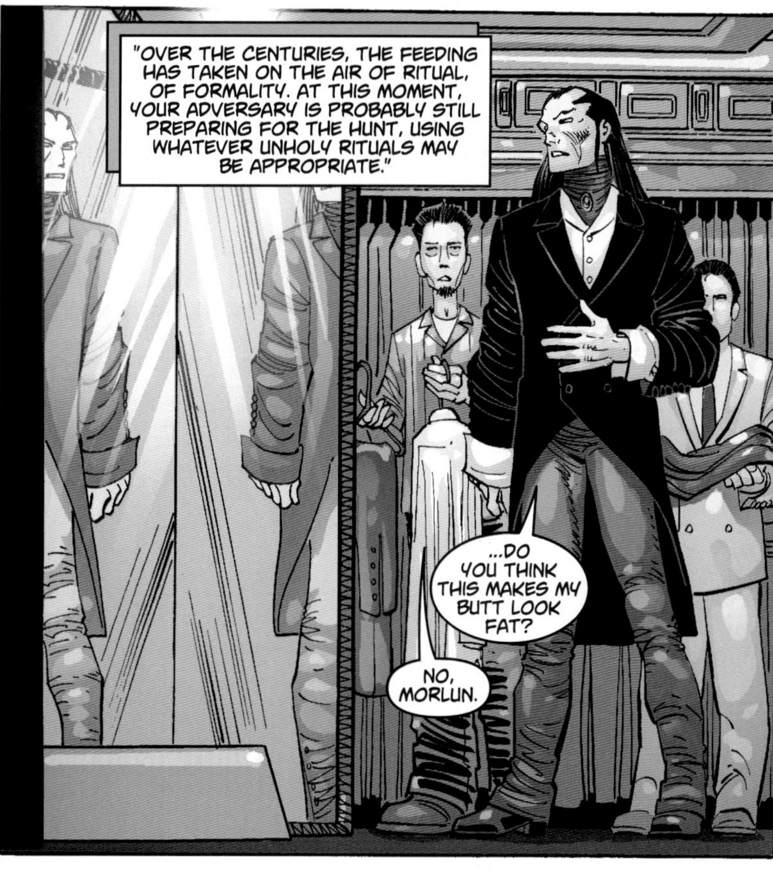
"OVER THE CENTURIES, THE FEEDING HAS TAKEN ON THE AIR OF RITUAL, OF FORMALITY. AT THIS MOMENT, YOUR ADVERSARY IS PROBABLY STILL PREPARING FOR THE HUNT, USING WHATEVER UNHOLY RITUALS MAY BE APPROPRIATE."
...DO YOU THINK THIS MAKES MY BUTT LOOK FAT?
NO, MORLUN.

SO HOW DOES THIS GUY --
MY PEOPLE BELIEVE HIS NAME IS MORLUN.
HOW DOES THIS MORLUN KNOW I'M THE ONE HE WANTS?

PETER...YOU DRESS LIKE A SPIDER. THIS WAS NOT YOUR BEST MOVE. I MEAN, YOU PUT THE SOURCE OF YOUR POWER RIGHT THERE ON YOUR CHEST.
OKAY --
WHAT IF CAPTAIN AMERICA CALLED HIMSELF SUPER-SERUM MAN, OR THE HULK WAS GAMMA-RAY MAN, OR --
ALL RIGHT, ALL RIGHT, JEEZ...
I WAS FIFTEEN YEARS OLD, CUT ME A LITTLE SLACK, HERE.

HERE YOU GO.
AND HERE'S ANOTHER THING... YOU WALK INTO MY LIFE, YOU GIVE ME GRIEF ABOUT WHAT I'VE DONE WITH IT... YOU CAN DO SOME OF THE THINGS I CAN DO. WHAT HAVE YOU DONE WITH IT?

YOU WANNA KNOW?
YEAH, I WANNA KNOW.
OKAY. C'MON.
GOOD.
TAXI!
...EEP!

YOU WORK IN THIS PLACE?
I OWN THIS PLACE.
HERE YOU GO. KEEP THE CHANGE.
...EEP!

GOOD AFTERNOON, MR. SIMS...
WELCOME BACK, MR. SIMS...
HOW YOU DOING, MR. SIMS...
GOT YOUR ELEVATOR RIGHT HERE, MR. SIMS...
AFTERNOON... THANKS.
THIS WAY.

HELTER SKELTER...HELTER SKELTER...
WAITAMINIT --

...DEE-DEE- DEE-DEE-DEE-DEE...HELTER SKELTER...
YOU'VE ACTUALLY GOT A MUZAK VERSION OF HELTER SKELTER?
I FIND IT KEEPS THE EMPLOYEES ON THEIR TOES.

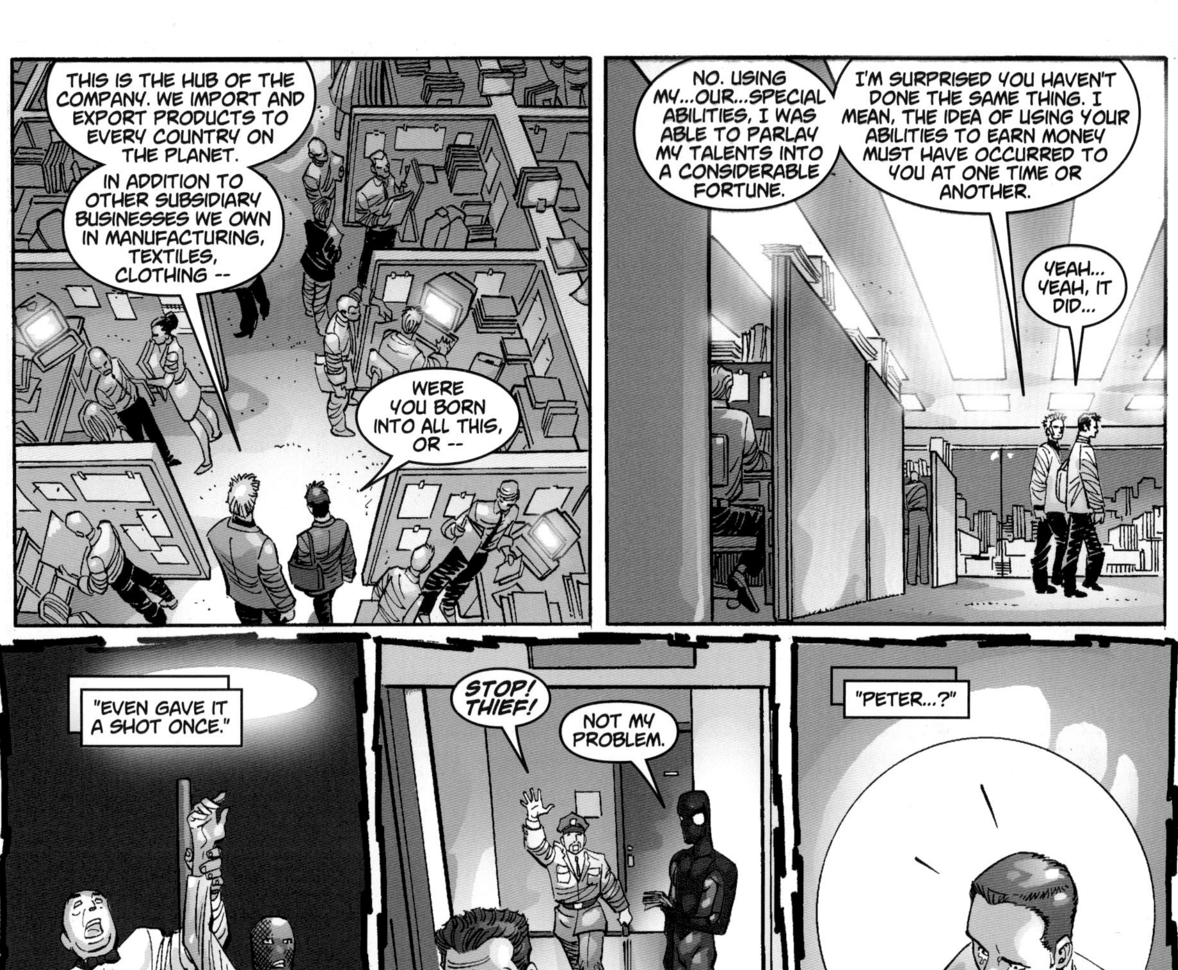
THIS IS THE HUB OF THE COMPANY. WE IMPORT AND EXPORT PRODUCTS TO EVERY COUNTRY ON THE PLANET.
IN ADDITION TO OTHER SUBSIDIARY BUSINESSES WE OWN IN MANUFACTURING, TEXTILES, CLOTHING --
WERE YOU BORN INTO ALL THIS, OR --
NO. USING MY...OUR...SPECIAL ABILITIES, I WAS ABLE TO PARLAY MY TALENTS INTO A CONSIDERABLE FORTUNE.
I'M SURPRISED YOU HAVEN'T DONE THE SAME THING. I MEAN, THE IDEA OF USING YOUR ABILITIES TO EARN MONEY MUST HAVE OCCURRED TO YOU AT ONE TIME OR ANOTHER.
YEAH... YEAH, IT DID...

"EVEN GAVE IT A SHOT ONCE."
STOP! THIEF!
NOT MY PROBLEM.
"SO WHAT HAPPENED?
"PETER...?"

IT'S... A LONG STORY. WHAT MATTERS IS THAT I LEARNED SOMETHING. SOMETHING MY UNCLE BEN TAUGHT ME.
WITH GREAT POWER THERE MUST ALSO COME GREAT RESPONSIBILITY.

UMM, HMM...
AND THEN WHAT?
AND THEN WHAT, WHAT?

"WITH GREAT POWER COMES GREAT RESPONSIBILITY."
RIGHT...
SO WHAT COMES WITH GREAT RESPONSIBILITY? WHAT'S THE OTHER HALF OF THE EQUATION? POWER? FREEDOM? GUILT?
I...I DON'T... I MEAN...

YOU ENJOY DOING THIS, DON'T YOU?
OF COURSE NOT.

THIS... IS YOUR OFFICE?
YOU APPROVE?
I'LL TAKE TWO.

UNFORTUNATELY, THE...OFFICE...I WOULD LIKE YOU TO CONSIDER HAS A BIT LESS OF A VIEW.
NONE AT ALL, TO BE PRECISE.
AN OFFICE?
PLEASE... STEP INSIDE.

I HAD MY BEST ENGINEERS WORKING ON THIS FOR ALMOST TWO YEARS. IT'S TWO FEET OF SOLID STEEL, WRAPPED AROUND AN ADAMANTIUM CORE. IT HAS SELF-CONTAINED RECYCLING SYSTEMS FOR AIR AND WATER, A FOUR MONTH SUPPLY OF FOOD BENEATH THE FLOOR.
FOR THE SAME AMOUNT OF MONEY, I COULD'VE BOUGHT A SMALL LATIN AMERICAN COUNTRY.

WHAT IS IT? SOME KIND OF BOMB SHELTER?
SOMETHING LIKE THAT. I BUILT IT FOR YOU. EVEN BEFORE I FINALLY FOUND OUT WHO *YOU* WERE. WELL, WHO HE WAS. SPIDER-MAN.
I HIRED SIX OF THE BEST PRIVATE INVESTIGATORS ON THE PLANET. HAD THEM ALL WORKING ON INDIVIDUAL PIECES, THEN COLLATED THE FINAL DATA MYSELF. NO ONE ELSE IN THE COMPANY KNOWS YOUR SECRET.

OVER THE YEARS, I'VE... DONE VERY WELL BY MYSELF, BY THE BOARD OF DIRECTORS, MY EMPLOYEES... BUT LATELY, I'VE BEGUN TO WONDER IF I COULD'VE USED MY ABILITIES TO DO WHAT YOU'VE DONE. MAKE A DIFFERENCE.
I ADMIRE YOU, PETER. I LOOK AT WHAT YOU'VE DONE AGAINST OVERWHELMING ODDS... AND I THINK... I'VE BLOWN IT. I'M FIFTY-SEVEN YEARS OLD, AND I'VE DONE NOTHING TO MAKE THE WORLD A BETTER PLACE.

WHAT I CAN DO, THOUGH... IS SAVE YOU. FROM MORLUN. I'VE DONE AS MUCH AS I CAN TO ENSURE THAT THIS ROOM IS DAMNED NEAR INDESTRUCTIBLE. IT'S RADIOACTIVELY NEUTRAL. I HOPE THAT WILL PREVENT HIM FROM BEING ABLE TO FIND YOU.
WITH LUCK, HE'LL THINK YOU'VE MOVED ON. BY THE TIME HE MAKES HIS WAY BACK HERE, MAYBE WE CAN... I DON'T KNOW...
EZEKIEL --

-- I'M...WELL, I'M FLATTERED THAT YOU'D DO ALL THIS. SPEND...ALL THIS. BUT I CAN'T JUST SIT IN HERE AND HIDE --
YOU CAN'T FIGHT HIM, PETER. OTHERS HAVE TRIED. THEY'VE ALL DIED. THE PART OF YOU THAT IS SPIDER WANTS TO HIDE FROM THIS, AND THAT'S THE CORRECT RESPONSE.
IF YOU TRY TO FIGHT HIM, HE'LL KILL YOU. I CAN'T PUT IT TO YOU ANY PLAINER THAN THAT. LET ME DO AT LEAST THIS MUCH WITH MY LIFE.

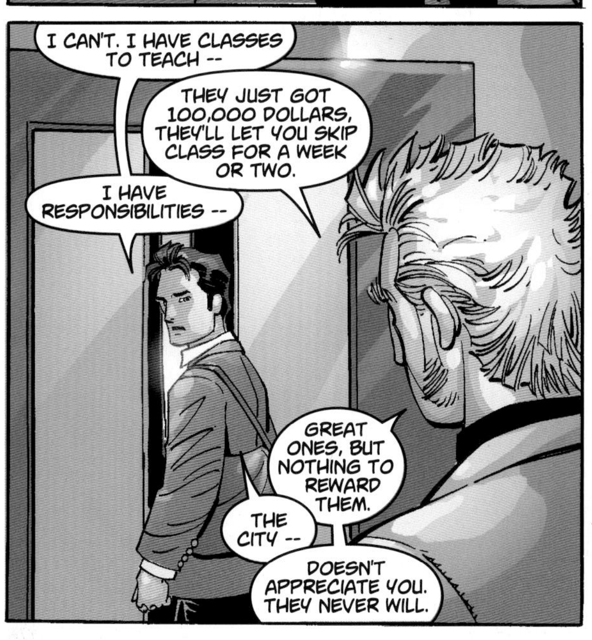
I CAN'T. I HAVE CLASSES TO TEACH --
THEY JUST GOT 100,000 DOLLARS, THEY'LL LET YOU SKIP CLASS FOR A WEEK OR TWO.
I HAVE RESPONSIBILITIES --
GREAT ONES, BUT NOTHING TO REWARD THEM.
THE CITY --
DOESN'T APPRECIATE YOU. THEY NEVER WILL.

LOOK, I APPRECIATE YOUR INTENTION, BUT I'M NOT GOING TO JUST HIDE FROM THIS GUY. WHO KNOWS WHAT HE'LL DO WHILE HE'S LOOKING FOR ME?
I'VE FACED GUYS BEFORE WHO SAID THEY WERE GOING TO KILL ME. HE ISN'T THE FIRST AND HE WON'T BE THE LAST. I'LL DEAL WITH IT.
PETER --

--LISTEN TO ME. YOU'VE NEVER FACED ANYONE... ANY*THING...* LIKE THIS BEFORE. HE'S BEEN DOING THIS FOR A THOUSAND YEARS. MAYBE LONGER. OTHERS LIKE YOU HAVE FACED HIM BEFORE.
NONE OF THEM SURVIVED.
HE *WILL* KILL YOU, PETER. AND I'D... I'D HATE TO SEE THAT HAPPEN. GIVE AN OLD MAN THE CHANCE TO DO FOR YOU WHAT YOU'VE DONE FOR OTHERS.

YOU KNOW WHAT COMES WITH GREAT RESPONSIBILITY, EZEKIEL?
WHAT?

ALL THAT.
GOOD NIGHT, EZEKIEL.

GOODBYE, PETER.

AS I WALK OUT OF THE BUILDING, I REALIZE THAT PETER PARKER HAS BEEN THE RECIPIENT OF A GREAT MANY KINDNESSES OVER THE YEARS.
SPIDER-MAN, ON THE OTHER HAND, HAS RECEIVED VERY FEW SUCH KINDNESSES. FOR A MOMENT THERE, IT WAS VERY NICE...TO BE ACCEPTED, TO BE OFFERED SANCTUARY.

BUT MOMENTS PASS.
IT'S WHAT THEY DO.

MORLUN...?

IS THERE ANYTHING YOU NEED? YOU'VE BEEN PRETTY QUIET SINCE WE GOT BACK. IS THERE ANYTHING I CAN --
NO. NOT ANYMORE.

I'M READY.

-- AND IT LOOKS LIKE ONCE AGAIN NOBODY IS GOING TO BE ABLE TO STOP THE YANKEES FROM HEADING FOR THE NEXT WORLD SERIES --
-- BZZZT --
WE INTERRUPT THIS BROADCAST FOR A SPECIAL BULLETIN.

REPORTS ARE COMING IN BY PHONE DESCRIBING A SCENE OF COMPLETE CARNAGE ON THE EAST SIDE, WE'VE DISPATCHED REPORTERS TO THE SCENE AND WE HOPE TO HAVE MORE INFORMATION TO YOU SHORTLY.

WE NOW RETURN YOU TO YOUR PREVIOUSLY SCHEDULED PROGRAM.

HELP! SOMEONE HELP!

HELLLLPPP!

I'VE GOT YOU! HANG ON!
ARE YOU ALL RIGHT, MA'AM?
YES, BUT --
AAAGGHH!
WHAT... ARE YOU ALL --
SPIDER-SENSE GOING NUTS... JUST LIKE BEFORE... SCREAMING HIDE --
-- HIDE --!
UNNGH!

I TASTE BLOOD AS I HIT THE CAR. NOTHING'S EVER HIT ME THAT HARD. NOT THE HULK. NOT THOR. NOBODY.
WELL, THAT WAS... THAT WAS --
AND FOR THE FIRST TIME, I DON'T HAVE A WISECRACK RIGHT AT HAND.
BECAUSE NOTHING'S FUNNY ANYMORE.

The Amazing Spider-Man #33
COVER ARTWORK

OKAY, QUICK INVENTORY WHILE MY HEAD'S STILL CLEARING.
ARRIVE IN TIME TO SAVE PEOPLE FROM FIRE. CHECK.
JUST BEEN HIT HARDER THAN ANYBODY'S EVER HIT ME BEFORE. CHECK.
BAD GUY STANDING THERE, WAITING FOR ME TO FIGHT BACK. CHECK.
WILLINGNESS TO OBLIGE?
BIG OL' CHECK.

UNGH!
HUNH!
YEAH!
NUTS...
UNF!

AGH --
CRUMMP

GOTTA BUY SOME TIME HERE. REGROUP.
Y'KNOW, MOST OF THE GUYS I FIGHT SPEND A LOT OF TIME TELLING ME WHY THEY'RE DOING IT --

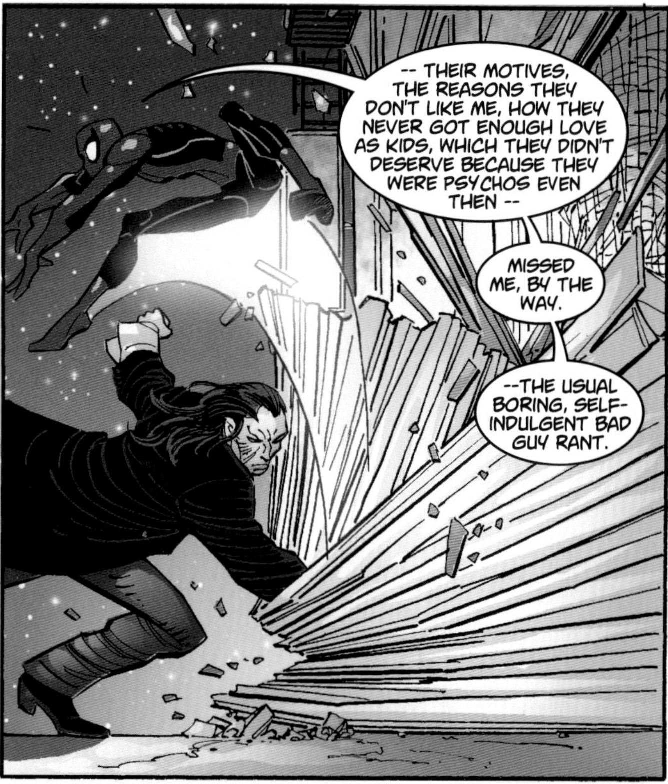
-- THEIR MOTIVES, THE REASONS THEY DON'T LIKE ME, HOW THEY NEVER GOT ENOUGH LOVE AS KIDS, WHICH THEY DIDN'T DESERVE BECAUSE THEY WERE PSYCHOS EVEN THEN --
MISSED ME, BY THE WAY.
--THE USUAL BORING, SELF-INDULGENT BAD GUY RANT.

SO, SUNSHINE, YOU GOT ANYTHING YOU WANT TO TELL OL' DOC SPIDEY? I PROMISE I'LL KEEP IT STRICTLY CONFIDENTIAL. JUST YOU AND ME, AND THE STAFF AT BELLEVUE.

I LIKE YOU. YOU'RE FUNNY.
DON'T TELL ME, TELL LETTERMAN.
I'VE BEEN TRYING TO GET ON HIS SHOW FOR YEARS.

OLIVIER
I HAVE NO SPECIAL DESIRE TO SEE YOU DEAD.

HERE IS HOW IT WILL HAPPEN.
YOU WILL RUN. I WILL PURSUE.
I DO NOT TIRE. I DO NOT GROW WEARY. I DO NOT GIVE UP.

YOU MAY GET AHEAD, BUT EVENTUALLY I WILL CATCH UP. NOW THAT I HAVE FOUND YOU, I WILL *ALWAYS* BE ABLE TO FIND YOU, WHEREVER YOU MAY HIDE.
THIS MAY TAKE HOURS OR DAYS. THE LONGEST WAS A WEEK. BUT IN TIME YOU WILL TIRE.
AND THEN YOU WILL DIE.

BUT I GIVE YOU MY SOLEMN WORD.
IT'S NOTHING PERSONAL.

SEE? ALREADY WE HAVE SOMETHING IN COMMON.
IT IS, HOWEVER, QUITE NECESSARY.
OH.

WAITAMINNIT... YOU'RE SAYING YOU'RE GONNA KILL ME AND IT'S NOTHING PERSONAL?
NOTHING *PERSONAL?*

LISTEN, BUDDY, I'VE FOUGHT EVERY KIND OF NUTBALL ON THE PLANET. I'VE FOUGHT FREAKS, MUTANTS, ALIENS AND HIGH-TECH GANGS... HECK, I'VE FOUGHT MY OWN ***COSTUME.***
AND YOU KNOW WHAT? YOU'RE THE FIRST ONE WHO'S REALLY TICKED ME OFF.
YOU ***WANT*** ME?

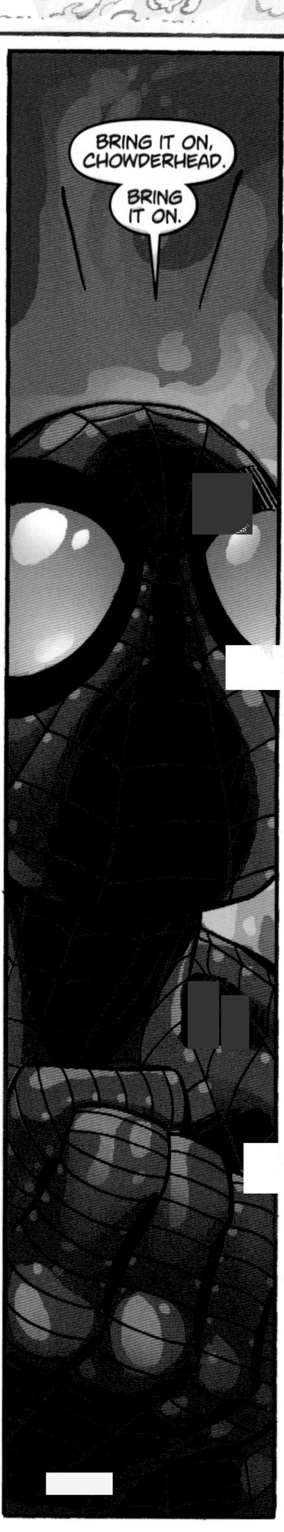
BRING IT ON, CHOWDERHEAD.
BRING IT ON.

I HIT HIM WITH EVERYTHING I'VE GOT.
HE KEEPS COMING.

I HIT HIM WITH EVERYTHING I CAN *FIND*.
HE KEEPS COMING.
HE DOESN'T TALK. HE DOESN'T SNARL. DOESN'T YELL, GLOAT, PREEN, CACKLE, THREATEN OR MOCK.
HE JUST KEEPS COMING.

SO I GO WHERE HE CAN'T. THIS TOE-TO-TOE STUFF IS FOR THE BIRDS.
BESIDES, BIRDS EAT SPIDERS.
YOU'RE LOOKING PRETTY WINDED THERE, SO I'LL JUST GO UP HERE AND --

-- GIVE YOU A --

-- BREAK...?
LOOK OUT!
NO...
WATCH IT!
OW!
HELP!
HE DOESN'T CARE WHO HE HURTS AS LONG AS HE GETS TO ME.

HAVE TO DRAW HIM AWAY FROM POPULATED AREAS. HE MAY BE ABLE TO CLIMB, BUT I'LL BET AUNT MAY'S FAVORITE CHAIR HE CAN'T... DO...
...THIS!

FIFTEEN STORIES UP AND TWO BLOCKS DOWN. THAT OUGHT TO BUY ME ENOUGH TIME TO FIGURE OUT HOW TO BEAT THIS GUY.

IT'S NOT LIKE HE SEEMS TO HAVE ANY SPECIAL POWERS. HE CAN'T BURST INTO FLAME, HE DOESN'T HAVE TENTACLES, WINGS, CROCODILE TEETH... I'LL BET HE DOESN'T EVEN HAVE AN AMERICAN EXPRESS CARD.
HE'S JUST REALLY STRONG.
REALLY, REALLY STRONG.

BUT SO AM I. AND UP HERE THERE'S NOBODY TO GET IN THE WAY, NO CIVILIANS TO --

CAN'T BE... NOBODY'S THAT --

-- FAST.
WHUNF!
HEY! HEY! HEEEEEYYY!!
WEB-SHOOTERS! CAN'T GET TO MY WEB-SHOOTERS!
ARE YOU INSANE?! WE'LL BOTH DIE!

NO.
JUST YOU.

GOT TO GET FREE...
GOT TO GET FREE...
GOT... TO... GET...

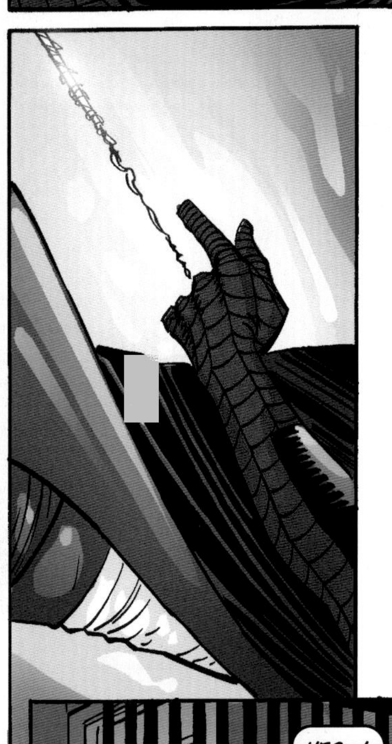

YES...!
YES!

UNNGH!

PPY BIR
NO... NO TICKERTAPE PARADE FOR ME NOW, THAT'S FINE... I'M JUST PROUD TO HAVE BEEN THE FIRST MAN TO WALK ON THE SUN...
I'LL... BE GOING NOW, THANKS EVER...

MISTER? MISTER, ARE YOU OKAY?
...GIVE ME... GIVE ME...
MY HAND?

YOUR SELF.
AIEEGH!

AIEEEEEEEE
NO!

LET -- HER --

-- GO!
NO MORE CIVILIANS, YOU HEAR ME?! THIS IS BETWEEN *US*, DAMN IT!
YOU WANT A FIGHT?
TOMMY

YOU'VE *GOT ONE!*
FALL.

FALL, DAMN YOU.
THROOM

FALL!

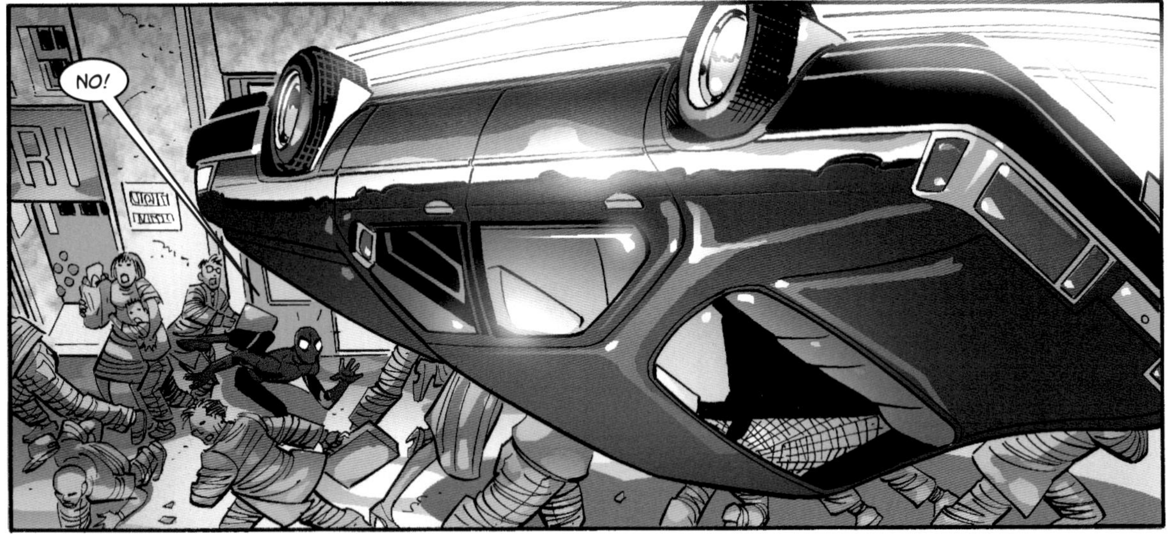
NO!

DOWN! GET DOWN!

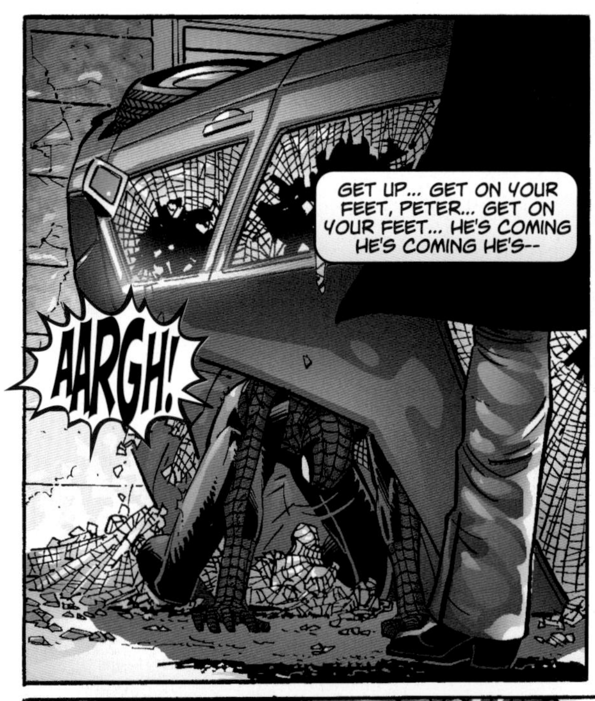
GET UP... GET ON YOUR FEET, PETER... GET ON YOUR FEET... HE'S COMING HE'S COMING HE'S--
AARGH!

AAGGHH!

CHEST ON FIRE... RIBS CRACKED... MAYBE BROKEN...

...CAN'T LET HIM KNOW... CAN'T...

SIRIC
PASTR

GOT TO PUT SOME ROOM BETWEEN US... DRAW HIM AWAY FROM THE CIVILIANS AGAIN.

HE KEEPS COMING... SILENT, SO SILENT. I FIND MYSELF ALMOST WISHING HE WOULD TAUNT ME... THAT HE'D SAY SOMETHING, ANYTHING...BECAUSE VANITY IS A WEAKNESS AND RIGHT NOW --

-- I DON'T SEE ANY OTHER WEAKNESSES.

MY ONLY CHANCE FOR NOW IS TO STAY AHEAD OF HIM AS MUCH AS I CAN.

THIS IS GONNA HURT --

-- REAL --

...BAD...

-- SO I'M TELLING YOU, PAUL, I SAID TO THIS GUY, THIS NETWORK WEASEL, I SAID, BUDDY, THIS IS A CONVERSATION THAT CAN ONLY END IN A GUNSHOT.

CLAP CLAP CLAP CLAP

LETTERMAN'S ON... SO WE'VE BEEN AT THIS FOR... THREE HOURS? HOW CAN HE KEEP GOING? THIS IS INSANE.

MAYBE IF SPIDER-MAN DISAPPEARS, HE'LL GO BACK TO WHEREVER HE GOES WHEN I'M NOT AROUND TO ATTACK.

I NEED JUST A LITTLE TIME TO CATCH MY BREATH, TO --

-- OH MAN... OH, THAT'S --

NO... COME ON, NO WAY, NO...

...WAY.
I SAID, NOW THAT I HAD FOUND YOU, I COULD ALWAYS FIND YOU.

DON'T SUPPOSE YOU'VE GOT A CAN OF SPINACH BACK THERE, DO YOU...?
HUH?
SIGH...SKIP IT...NOBODY WATCHES CARTOONS ANYMORE...

HE DOESN'T GET TIRED... ONLY GETS STRONGER AS HE GOES... BUT HE KNOWS I'M EXHAUSTED--

AND DAMN HIM, HE KNOWS EXACTLY WHAT IT TAKES TO PULL ME IN AGAIN.

I WON'T LET AN INNOCENT BE HURT.

BUT I'M AN INNOCENT TOO, AREN'T I?

WHAT DID I DO... THAT I SHOULD DIE LIKE THIS?

NO... YOU'RE NOT GOING TO DIE, PETER. YOU'RE NOT GOING TO DIE AND YOU'RE NOT GOING TO KEEP LETTING HIM DO WHATEVER HE WANTS --
-- TO WHOMEVER HE WANTS.
YOU'VE GOT THE COSTUME. YOU'VE GOT THE POWER.

YOU'RE SPIDER-MAN.
ACT LIKE IT.

GREAT POWER.
GREAT RESPONSIBILITY.

AND A GREAT LEFT HOOK.

OKAY...OKAY, PAL...THIS IS WHERE YOU GET YOUR --

OH, NO --

-- GAS!

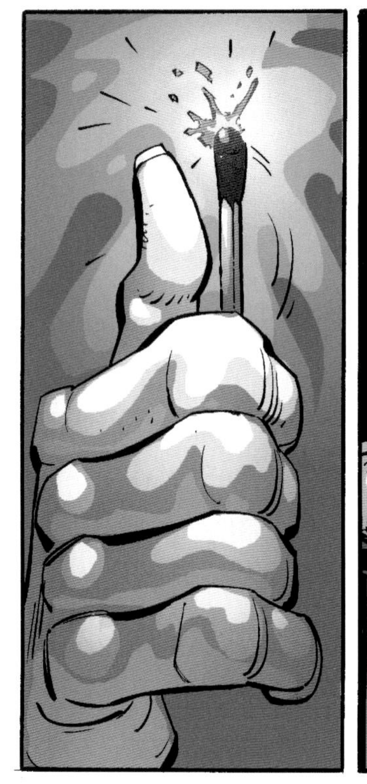

TOO FAR... NOT GOING TO REACH IT IN TIME...

STUPID... THOUGHT HE'D KILL US BOTH, HE ONLY GOT HIMSELF, ONLY --

...NO...

ONE CHANCE... ONE PERSON WHO CAN HELP... JUST HAVE TO GET THERE IN ONE PIECE.

FRESH CLOTHES, DEX.
YES, MORLUN.
HE'S GOOD. JUST...
WHAT, MORLUN?

THERE'S SOMETHING... WRONG ABOUT HIM. STILL, HE HAS WHAT I REQUIRE, AND THAT IS ALL THAT MATTERS.
IT'S ALL THAT HAS EVER MATTERED.

KRAACK
EZEKIEL...YOU KNOW MORE ABOUT THIS MORLUN THAN I DO...I NEED YOUR HELP...

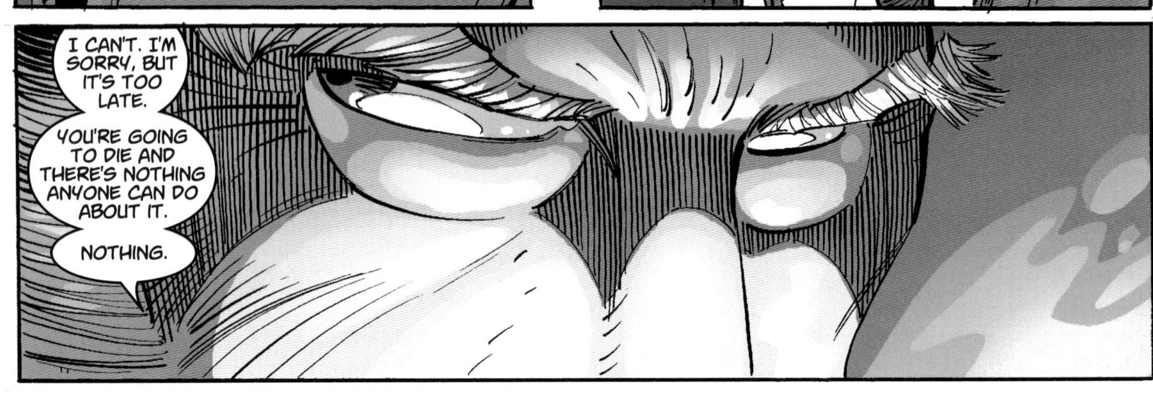
I CAN'T. I'M SORRY, BUT IT'S TOO LATE.
YOU'RE GOING TO DIE AND THERE'S NOTHING ANYONE CAN DO ABOUT IT.
NOTHING.

The Amazing Spider-Man #34
Cover Artwork

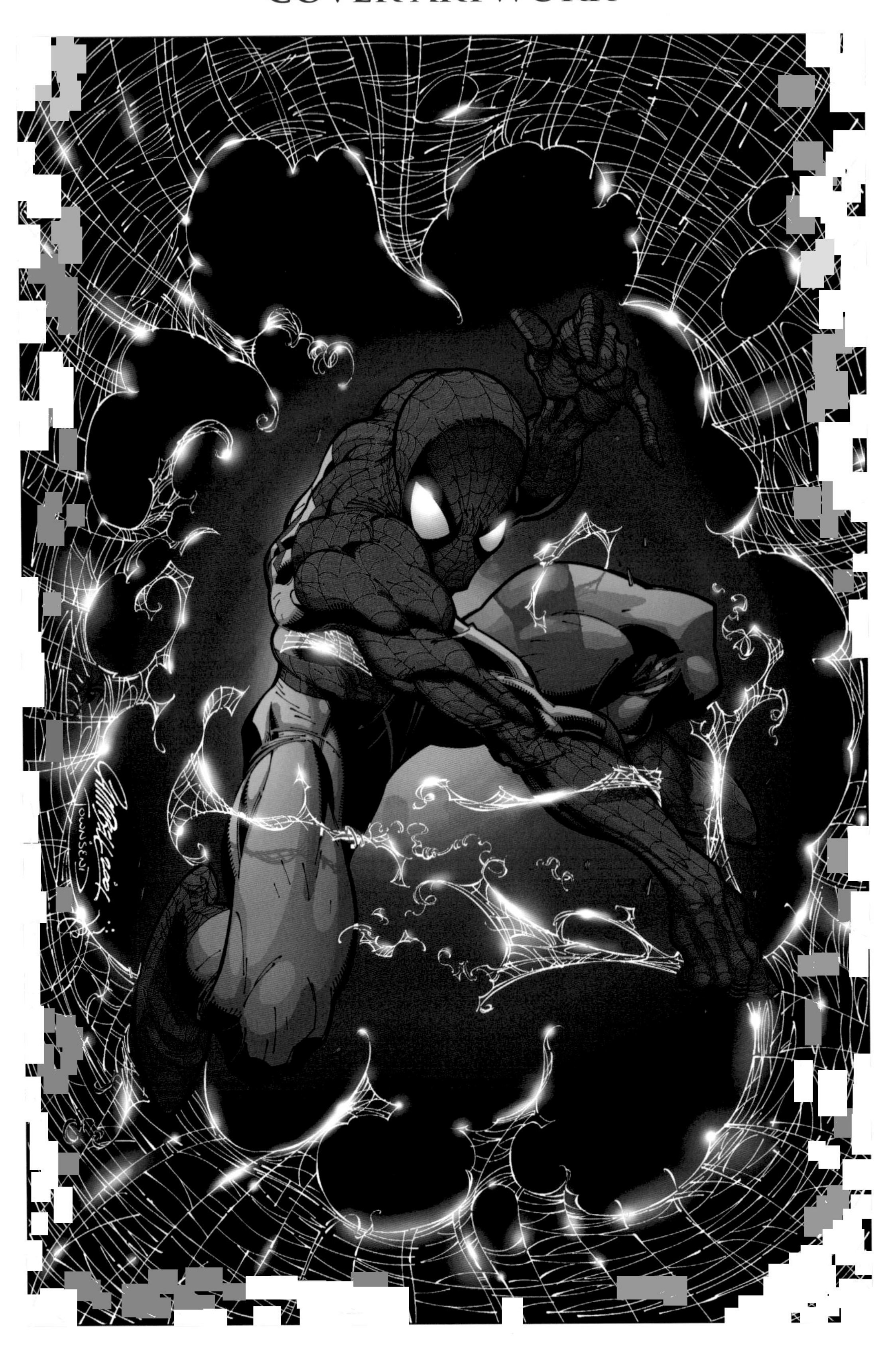

THE UNIVERSE GIVETH AND THE UNIVERSE TAKETH AWAY.
SIMMS

BUT RIGHT NOW THE UNIVERSE SEEMS TO BE SPENDING A LOT MORE TIME TAKETHING THAN GIVETHING.
THIS PLACE WAS SUPPOSED TO BE A SHELTER AGAINST MORLUN, THE GUY WHO'S SMEARED ME ACROSS MOST OF NEW YORK CITY.
NOW EZEKIEL TELLS ME IT'S USELESS.
AND THE HITS JUST KEEP ON COMING.
WHAT DO YOU MEAN IT'S TOO LATE?

THIS SHELTER -- ADAMANTIUM ALLOYS, THE AIR RECYCLING SYSTEM, THE REINFORCED STEEL SKIN -- WAS DESIGNED TO HELP KEEP MORLUN FROM FINDING YOU. IN TIME, HE WOULD HAVE GIVEN UP AND GONE ELSEWHERE.
BUT ONCE HE TOUCHED YOU... ALL THIS BECAME IRRELEVANT. HE CAN FIND YOU WHEREVER YOU GO.

YOU CANNOT RUN. YOU CANNOT HIDE.
YOU CAN ONLY FIGHT. AND EVENTUALLY DIE.
THAT'S IT. I'M SORRY.
SWELL.

WHAT HAPPENED TO "WE HAVE SIMILAR POWERS BUT I'M GETTING OLD AND I WANT TO DO ONE LAST GOOD THING WITH MY LIFE"?
I MADE YOU AN OFFER. YOU DECLINED.
OKAY, I GOT THAT PART, I'M PAST THAT. YOU KNOW WHAT I'M UP AGAINST. HOW ABOUT A HELPING HAND?

I CAN'T. YOU'RE THE MAIN TARGET, THE ONE ON WHOM HE CAN MOST FULLY FEED. THE PURER THE SOURCE, THE MORE HE CAN ABSORB.
BUT I'M CLOSE ENOUGH TO BE A PRETTY DECENT APPETIZER. THAT'S WHY I'VE BEEN CAREFUL TO AVOID HIM. SO FAR I DON'T THINK HE EVEN KNOWS I EXIST.

I CAN'T RISK EXPOSING MYSELF TO HIM, NOT EVEN FOR YOU.
THEN AT LEAST GIVE ME SOMETHING I CAN USE.

I'VE NEVER ASKED FOR MUCH. LIKE EVERYBODY ELSE, I KNOW THE ODDS ARE ALWAYS AGAINST US. THAT'S JUST THE WAY THE UNIVERSE WORKS. I DON'T WANT GUARANTEES, PROMISES, ASSURANCES OR FALSE HOPES.
ALL I'VE EVER ASKED IS FOR ONE CHANCE TO TRY, TO STAND ON MY OWN FEET AND GIVE IT MY BEST SHOT. SUCCEED OR FAIL, LIVE OR DIE, IF I KNOW I TRIED, THEN I CAN ACCEPT WHATEVER HAPPENS.

I'M SORRY, PETE. I HAVE MORE MONEY THAN I EVER WANTED. I CAN BUY YOU ANYTHING YOU WANT.
BUT I CAN'T GIVE YOU THIS. I DON'T KNOW ANY WAY TO STOP MORLUN, LET ALONE BEAT HIM.

YOU'RE ON YOUR OWN.

WELL... IT WON'T BE THE FIRST TIME.

GOODBYE, EZEKIEL.

AS I TRY TO KEEP MY CRACKED RIBS FROM GRINDING, I WEIGH MY REMAINING OPTIONS THAT DON'T INVOLVE GETTING TURNED INTO A WET SPOT ON THE CONCRETE.
OPTION ONE: I CAN GET ON A PLANE AND GET OUT OF THE COUNTRY. BUT THERE'S NO TELLING HOW MUCH DAMAGE HE'LL DO ONCE HE REALIZES I'M GONE... TO TRY AND PULL ME BACK AGAIN.
OPTION TWO...

OPTION TWO...
DAMN... THERE'S NEVER A GOOD OPTION TWO AROUND WHEN YOU REALLY NEED ONE. AND WORST OF ALL...

I THINK HE'S DECIDED NOT TO WAIT AROUND FOR ME TO SHOW UP AGAIN.

I CAN'T... I HAVE OBLIGATIONS.
I HAVE RESPONSIBILITIES.
I HAVE A BOARD OF DIRECTORS AND SHAREHOLDERS AND ACCOUNTANTS AND ANNUAL REPORTS AND AN ITINERARY.
I HAVE...

...TO GO TO WORK NOW.

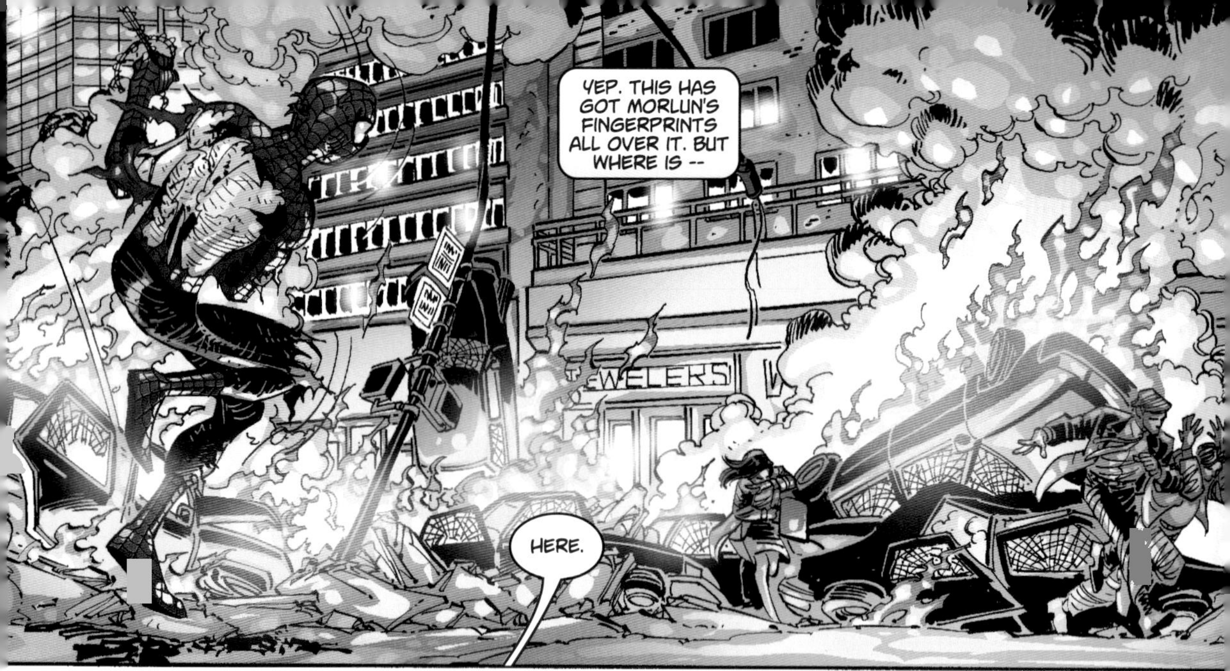
YEP. THIS HAS GOT MORLUN'S FINGERPRINTS ALL OVER IT. BUT WHERE IS --
HERE.

I SEE HIM... I SEE HE HAS... AND IN THAT INSTANT THE PAIN IS GONE, THE FATIGUE IS GONE, EVERYTHING IS GONE WITH ONE EXCEPTION.

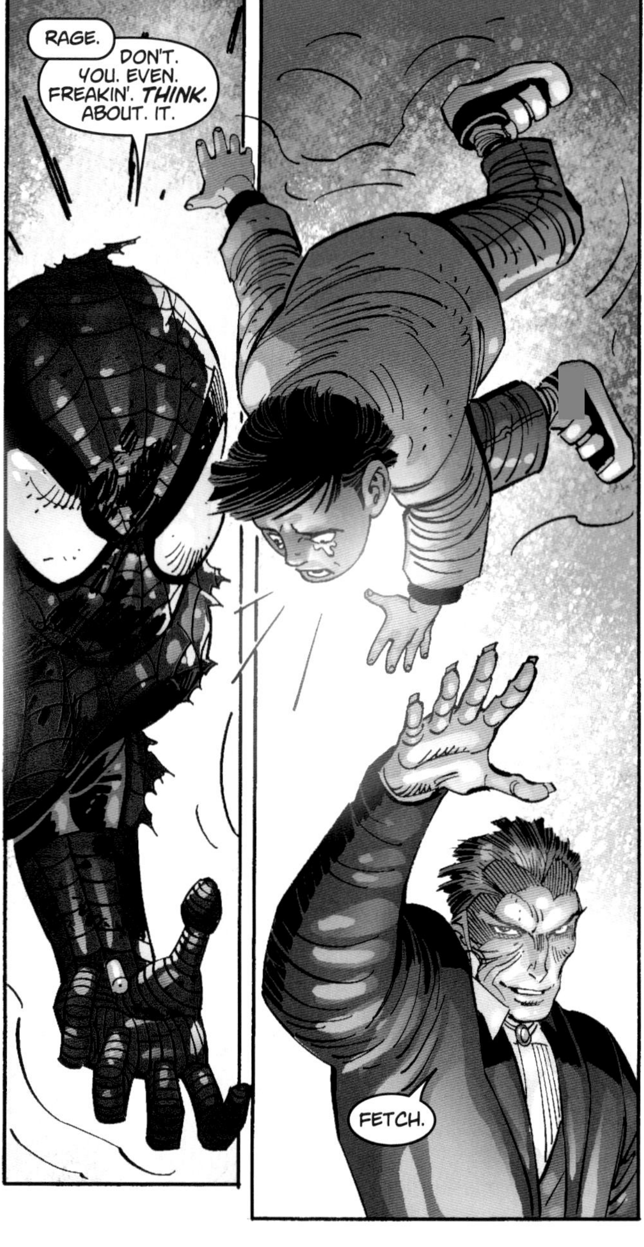
RAGE.
DON'T. YOU. EVEN. FREAKIN'. THINK. ABOUT. IT.
FETCH.

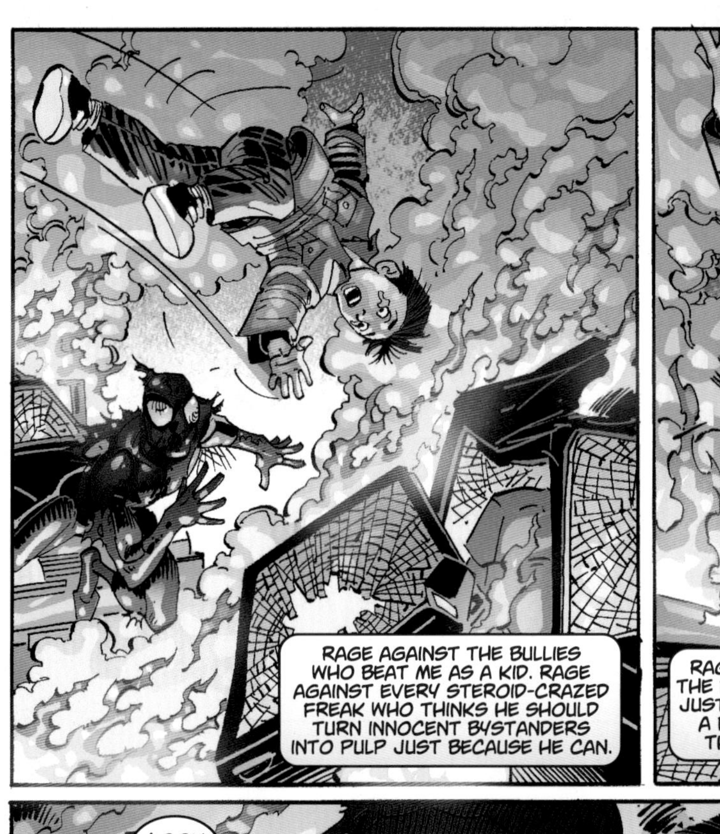
RAGE AGAINST THE BULLIES WHO BEAT ME AS A KID. RAGE AGAINST EVERY STEROID-CRAZED FREAK WHO THINKS HE SHOULD TURN INNOCENT BYSTANDERS INTO PULP JUST BECAUSE HE CAN.

RAGE AGAINST THE PEOPLE WHO JUST DON'T GIVE A DAMN WHO THEY HURT.
GOT YOU!

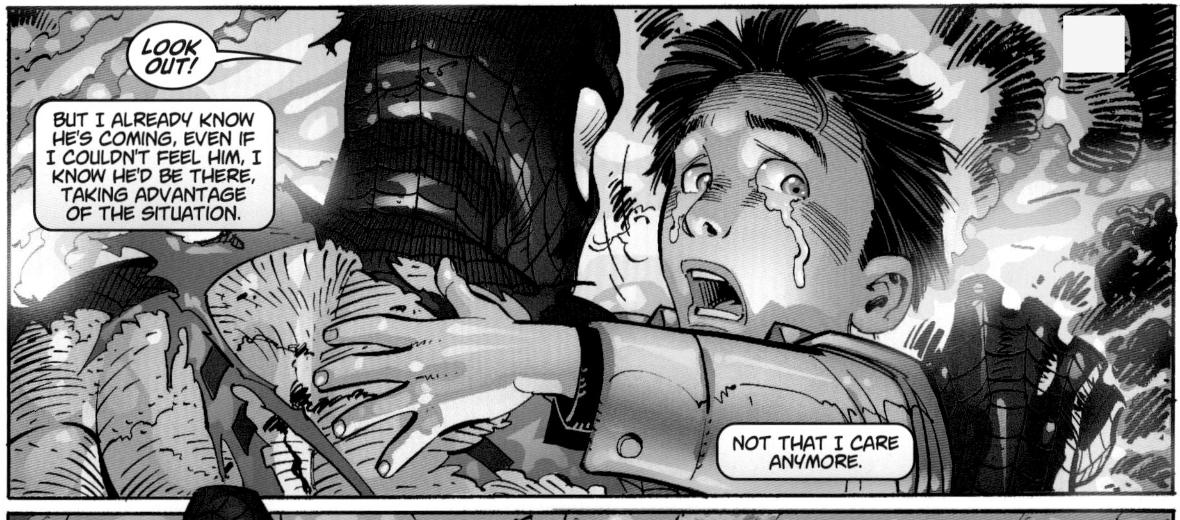
LOOK OUT!
BUT I ALREADY KNOW HE'S COMING, EVEN IF I COULDN'T FEEL HIM, I KNOW HE'D BE THERE, TAKING ADVANTAGE OF THE SITUATION.
NOT THAT I CARE ANYMORE.

I JUST WANT A PIECE OF THE CREEP.

I GET IN SOME GOOD SHOTS. HE BARELY FEELS THEM.

BUT I FEEL EVERY ONE OF HIS. DOESN'T MATTER.

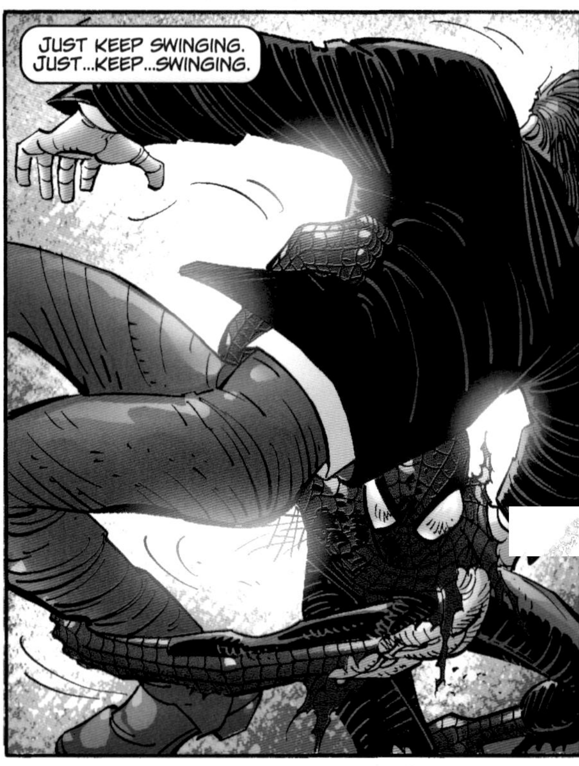
JUST KEEP SWINGING. JUST...KEEP...SWINGING.

THIS PROBABLY WON'T WORK. BUT I'VE GOTTA TRY EVERYTHING.
NOT THAT YOU NEED A FASHION CONSULTANT OR ANYTHING...WELL, MAYBE A GOOD PSYCHOLOGIST... AND AS MUCH AS I LIKE A GOOD GOTH COAT --

-- I THINK IT JUST NEEDS SOMETHING A LITTLE EXTRA. WEBBING, MAYBE.
I POUR IT ON, RUNNING BOTH WEB-SHOOTERS DOWN TO HALF-CAPACITY.

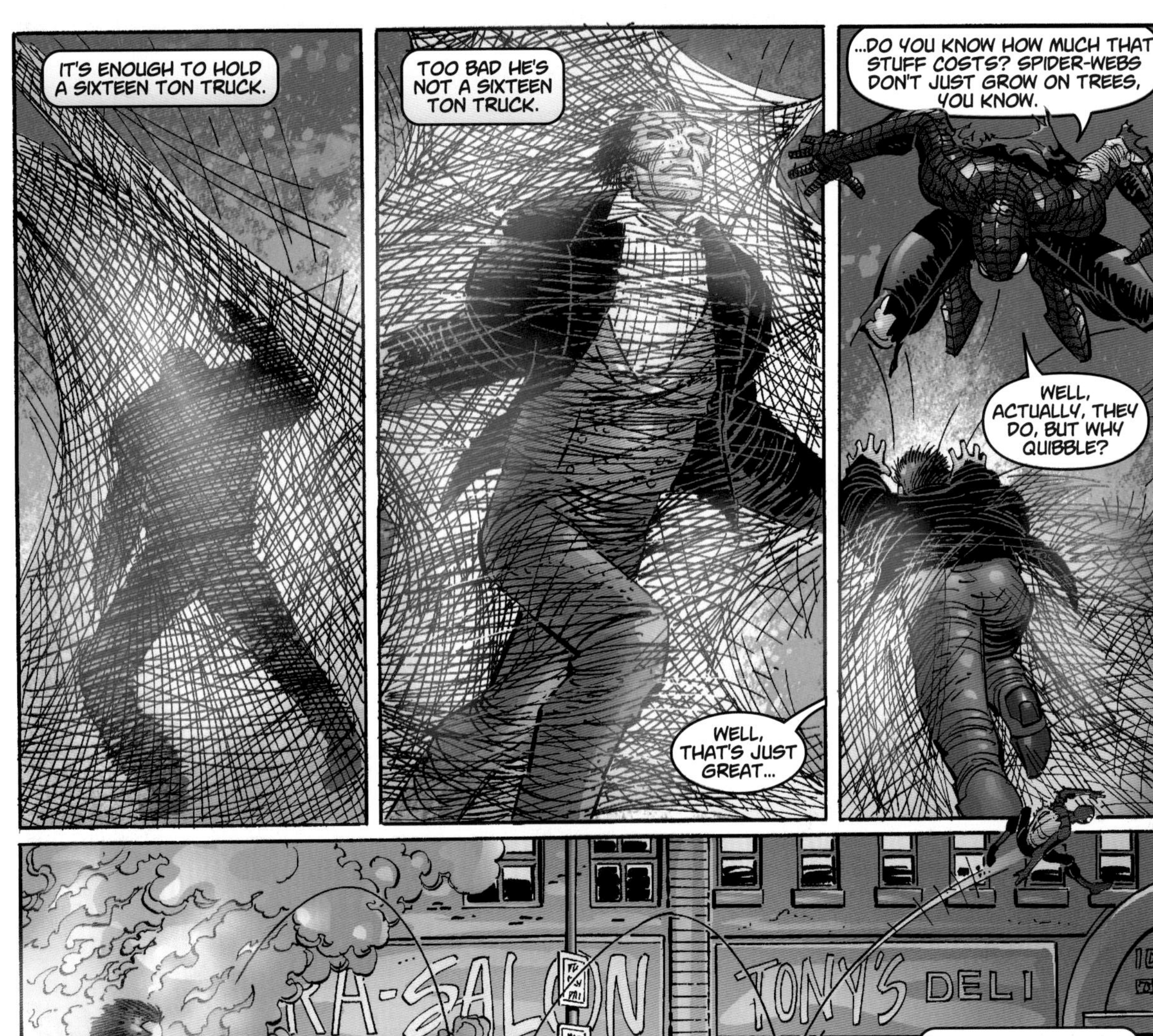
IT'S ENOUGH TO HOLD A SIXTEEN TON TRUCK.
TOO BAD HE'S NOT A SIXTEEN TON TRUCK.
WELL, THAT'S JUST GREAT...
...DO YOU KNOW HOW MUCH THAT STUFF COSTS? SPIDER-WEBS DON'T JUST GROW ON TREES, YOU KNOW.
WELL, ACTUALLY, THEY DO, BUT WHY QUIBBLE?

RA-SALON
TONY'S
DELI
HE ONLY GOES NUTS WHEN I GET TOO FAR AHEAD. SO THE KEY IS TO STAY JUST FAR ENOUGH AHEAD TO BUY TIME WITHOUT FORCING HIM TO GO AFTER OTHERS TO SLOW ME DOWN OR BRING ME BACK.

JUST ONE THING I'M GONNA NEED.

BUT THE LACK OF POCKETS STRIKES AGAIN.

THWIP
BLIND! PLEASE GIVE!

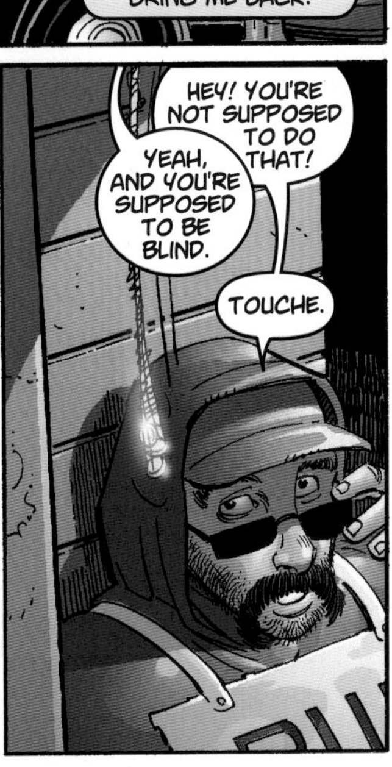
HEY! YOU'RE NOT SUPPOSED TO DO THAT!
YEAH, AND YOU'RE SUPPOSED TO BE BLIND.
TOUCHE.

-- AND THE THING ABOUT MR. PARKER IS, HE *WANTS* TO BE HERE. SOME OF THE OTHER TEACHERS, IT'S LIKE THEY HAVE TO BE HERE BECAUSE THEY CAN'T DO ANYTHING ELSE. BUT HE'S LIKE --
YES? OH, HELLO, MR. PARKER.

OH, I'M SORRY YOU CAN'T MAKE IT IN TODAY. YES, EVERY TEACHER HAS FOUR SICK DAYS, BUT USUALLY THEY SAVE THEM FOR AFTER THEY'VE BEEN TEACHING FOR A WHILE...
NO, I DON'T THINK THAT WAS AN ATTEMPT AT COMMENTARY, JUST AN OBSERVATION.

IT'S JUST THAT MOST *REAL* SICKNESSES START THE NIGHT BEFORE, NOT AN HOUR BEFORE CLASS, SO --
THANK YOU FOR THE SUGGESTION, BUT I DON'T THINK THAT'S ANATOMICALLY POSSIBLE, MR. PARKER.
EXIT

EEEEEEEEEEEEEEEEEEEEEE
I CAN HEAR THE SCREAMS STARTING AGAIN EVEN AS I HANG UP THE PHONE, AND I KNOW IT'S HIM, DRAWING ME OUT AGAIN... AND I THINK...
AM I THAT PREDICTABLE?

I'M TIRED. I'VE BEEN FIGHTING THIS GUY FOR NEARLY TWELVE HOURS STRAIGHT, I HAVEN'T HAD ANYTHING TO EAT OR DRINK... AND HE'S NOT EVEN TIRED.
BUT I AM. I'M HURT AND I'M TIRED AND I WANT TO GO HOME AND I WANT TO SLEEP AND I DON'T WANT TO BE HERE... AND I THINK...
CAN I LET THIS ONE GO? CAN I LET IT BE SOMEONE ELSE'S PROBLEM, JUST FOR A MINUTE, SO I CAN REST?

NO. I CAN'T.
BUT I WISH I COULD. GOD, BUT I WISH I COULD.

PLEASE! I... I DIDN'T DO ANYTHING, PLEASE!
PLEASE SCREAM AGAIN. I DON'T BELIEVE HE HEARD YOU.
I HEARD, ALL RIGHT.

WHOMP
UNGH!

COME ON, THAT HAD TO HURT.
MAYBE THAT'S THE WAY TO BEAT HIM, KEEP HIM AT ARM'S LENGTH, WHERE HE CAN'T REACH ME, AND WEAR HIM DOWN.

NO PARKING
IT'S A GREAT THEORY.

BUT THE WEARING DOWN PART DOESN'T SEEM TO BE WORKING OUT AS WELL AS I'D HOPED FOR.

HEY! LEGGO, THAT'S MY --
UH, OH... WHAT'S HE --
NO!
THE WALL! I'M TOO CLOSE TO THE W--

AAAGHHH!

CAN'T BREATHE... GOD, I CAN'T BREATHE... CHEST'S ON FIRE... CAN'T MOVE....

COME ON, PETER... MOVE... MOVE!
AS I TOLD YOU, I REGRET THE NECESSITY OF THIS. YOU HAVE FOUGHT WELL, IF BRIEFLY.

BRIEFLY? BRIEFLY?! BRIEFLY MY DEAR AUNT FANNY.
...SCREW...

...YOU...

GOT IT!

AGH! AGGHH...
NYC RUL

AGGHH...

YOU SEEM RATHER DISTRACTED, SIR.

HMM? OH, SORRY... NOTHING. YOU WERE SAYING --

I WAS SAYING THAT WE CAN MAXIMIZE OUR REVENUE STREAMS BY CONSOLIDATING THE OFFSHORE ACCOUNTS.

FURTHER, IF WE EXPAND THE FACILITIES AT MAZATLAN USING A LINE OF CREDIT INSTEAD OF SPENDING REAL MONIES, WE CAN USE THE CAPITAL TO...

NOT MUCH MONEY LEFT...

...I COULD TRY CALLING THE FF, BUT IF THEY'RE NOT IN TOWN... AND WHY THE HECK AREN'T MORE SUPER HEROES IN THE PHONE BOOK ANYWAY...
...DON'T BLACK OUT, DON'T BLACK OUT, YOU CAN'T AFFORD THAT...
THINK.

LIBERTY

RING... RING... RING...
C'MON, ANSWER --
RING... CLICK
HI --
MJ? MJ, IT'S ME, IT'S --
phone

THIS IS MARY JANE, I'M AWAY FROM THE PHONE RIGHT NOW, BUT IF YOU'LL LEAVE YOUR NAME AND NUMBER I'LL GET BACK TO YOU AS SOON AS POSSIBLE.

phone

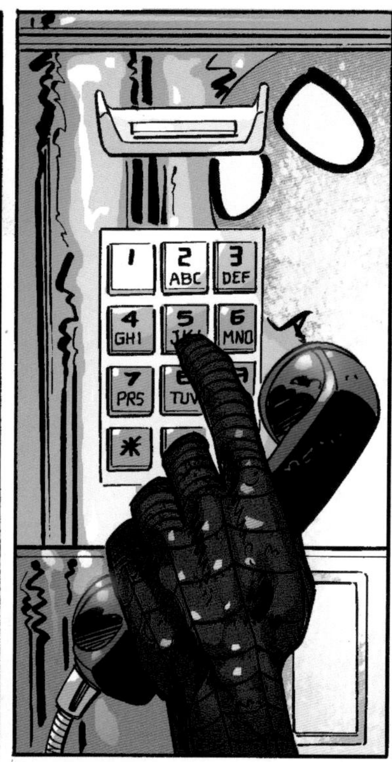

RING...RING...
CLICK
HELLO?
HI, IT'S ME.

PETER? ARE YOU ALL RIGHT?
YEAH... YEAH, AUNT MAY, I'M FINE --
YOU SOUND TERRIBLE. ARE YOU COMING DOWN WITH SOMETHING?
YEAH... I DUNNO... MAYBE... I'M JUST TIRED, THAT'S ALL. WANTED TO SEE HOW YOU WERE.
YOU'RE SO SWEET... ALWAYS LOOKING OUT FOR EVERYBODY ELSE.

I'M FINE, FINE. I'M GOING TO BE DROPPING OFF MY SPRING CLOTHES AT THE CLEANER'S TOMORROW MORNING. IF YOU LIKE, I COULD STOP BY YOUR PLACE AND PICK UP YOURS TOO ON THE WAY OUT.
OUT WITH THE WINTER CLOTHES, IN WITH THE SUMMER, RIGHT?
RIGHT... RIGHT... I... LISTEN, AUNT MAY --
PETER...?

YOU KNOW I LOVE YOU, RIGHT? I MEAN, I GET BUSY SOMETIMES, AND I MAY FORGET TO SAY IT, BUT I NEVER FORGET TO THINK IT.
YOU'RE MY FAVORITE AUNT IN THE WORLD, MAY. AND I LOVE YOU. WHATEVER HAPPENS, REMEMBER THAT.
PETER? I --

PLEASE DEPOSIT ANOTHER TWENTY-FIVE CENTS FOR THREE MINUTES.
I HAVE... I HAVE TO GO NOW. I'LL TALK TO YOU LATER.
PETER, WAIT, I --
TAKE CARE OF YOURSELF.

YOU TOO, PETER.
CLICK
I ALWAYS KNEW THAT SOONER OR LATER, I'D LOSE. IT'S MATH, YOU SEE. STATISTICS. NO ONE WINS FOREVER.
NO ONE.
ONLY THING THAT MATTERS IS HOW YOU FACE IT WHEN THE CARDS DON'T COME UP YOUR WAY.
I'M NOT AFRAID.
I'M TIRED, BUT I'M NOT AFRAID.
JUST SO YOU KNOW...

...I WON'T GO DOWN EASY.
AND THIS I SWEAR TO YOU... I WILL NOT GO DOWN ALONE.

...WON'T GIVE UP...
WON'T GIVE UP...
WON'T GIVE UP...
WON'T GIVE UP...
WON'T GIVE UP...
WON'T...

...WON'T
...GGGGGGGG...

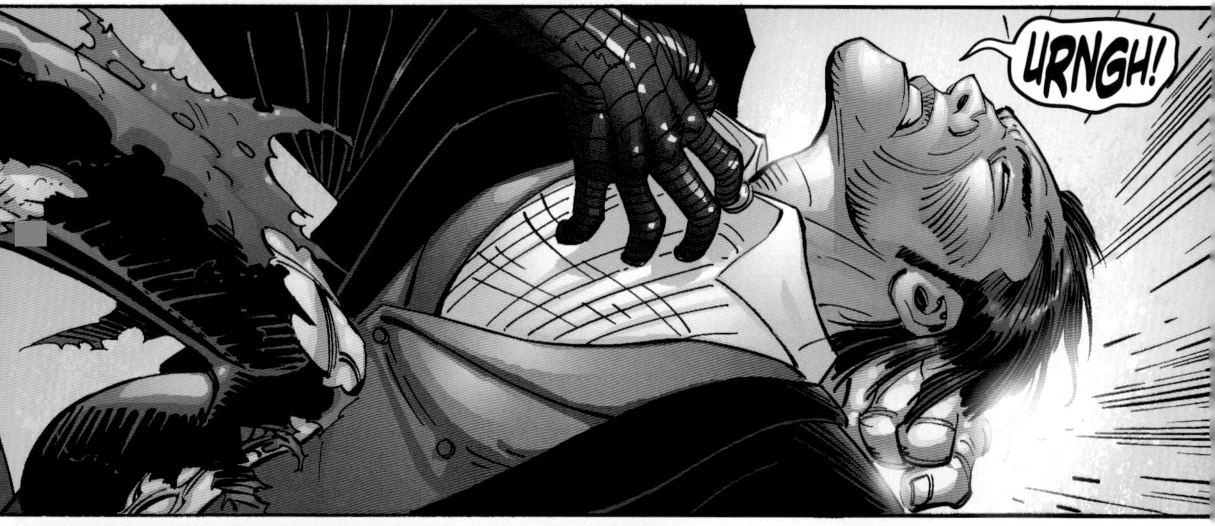
URNGH!

WHAT --
IT'S OKAY, P.

I CHANGED MY MIND.
IT'S A MOMENT... A MOMENT WHEN EVEN MORLUN SEEMS TAKEN ABACK.
AND IN THAT MOMENT, ODDLY ENOUGH, I FINALLY UNDERSTAND WHAT IT FEELS LIKE FOR SOMEONE ELSE TO LOOK UP AND SEE ME.
AND IT'S GREAT. TOTALLY, FREAKIN' GREAT.
BUT I ALSO KNOW THAT HE'S RISKED IT ALL BY TOUCHING MORLUN, WHO CAN NOW FIND EZEKIEL AT WILL IF I FAIL TO STOP HIM.

SO I'M JUST GONNA HAVE TO MAKE SURE THAT DOESN'T HAPPEN.
HEY!
DIDN'T YOUR MOTHER EVER TELL YOU NOT TO TURN YOUR BACK ON PEOPLE? IT'S RUDE.

IT'S JUST THE WAY OF THINGS, P. NOBODY'S GOT ANY CLASS THESE DAYS.

INTERESTING. YOU'RE NOT PURE. NOT LIKE HIM.
BUT I WILL TAKE YOU ANYWAY.
WASTE NOT, WANT NOT.

WE GO AT HIM TOGETHER. IT'S A NEW EXPERIENCE, RELYING ON SOMEONE WITH SIMILAR POWERS TO WHAT I HAVE.
HIS INSTINCTS ARE THE SAME AS MINE, HIS MOVEMENTS MUCH LIKE MY OWN, IT'S LIKE FIGHTING SIDE BY SIDE WITH AN OLDER VERSION OF MYSELF.
I THINK MY UNCLE BEN WOULD'VE LIKED HIM. I THINK THEY WOULD'VE HAD A LOT IN COMM--

UNGH!
YES!

NO! LET HIM GO!
IT'S NOT FAIR! LET HIM GO! LET - HIM --

GO!

I'M SORRY... PETE... I THOUGHT I COULD HOLD MY OWN... I THOUGHT...

I'M SORRY...

EZEKIEL!
NO!

NICE...NOT FILLING, BUT NICE...THINK I'LL GO HAVE A CAPPUCCINO NOW, JUST TO WASH THAT DOWN...
MONSTER!

CATCH UP WITH YOU LATER.

I KEEP DIVING FOR OVER TWENTY MINUTES, LONGER THAN EVEN I CAN HOLD MY BREATH.

NOTHING.

HE CAME AND HE HELPED AND HE FOUGHT AND HE DIED AND IT WAS ALL FOR NOTHING. ALL FOR...

NO... MAYBE NOT...

BECAUSE EZEKIEL TOOK MORLUN OFF GUARD, HE WAS ABLE TO TAG HIM ONCE, REAL GOOD. JUST ONCE, BUT IT WAS ENOUGH.
ENOUGH TO MAKE HIM BLEED. UP UNTIL NOW, MORLUN'S KNOWN ALL HE NEEDS TO KNOW ABOUT ME, BUT I'VE KNOWN NOTHING ABOUT MORLUN.

THAT JUST CHANGED.

I DON'T KNOW HOW MUCH TIME I HAVE, HOW MUCH TIME EZEKIEL BOUGHT ME. BUT HE GOT ME SOMETHING EVEN MORE IMPORTANT THAN TIME. SOMETHING I DIDN'T HAVE UNTIL NOW.

HE BOUGHT ME A CHANCE.
AND THAT'S ALL I'VE EVER NEEDED. JUST A CHANCE.
I MAY NOT BE REED RICHARDS, BUT BY GOD I'M A SCIENTIST, AND I'VE GOT THE EQUIPMENT TO PROVE IT. OKAY, MOST OF IT CAME FROM CATALOGS, BUT STILL --
AH-HA!
HIS BLOOD IS AN AMALGAM OF EVERY KIND OF CELL: ANIMAL, BIRD, HUMAN AND INSECT. PUREST FORMS OF DNA I'VE EVER SEEN.
THAT EXPLAINS HOW HE CAN GO AFTER ME OR ANYONE ELSE EZEKIEL DESCRIBED AS A TOTEM.
MY GUESS IS THAT THE CELLS BREAK DOWN OVER TIME AND REQUIRE PERIODIC RECHARGING FROM A SOURCE LIFE-FORM IN EACH CATEGORY.

THE PURER THE SOURCE, THE STRONGER THE CHARGE.
THAT'S WHY HE WANTS ME. EZEKIEL THINKS THAT I'M CLOSER TO THIS TOTEMISTIC SOURCE.
TRUTH IS, I'VE NEVER ENTIRELY ACCEPTED HIS STORY.
MAYBE IT'S TRUE. MAYBE IT ISN'T. I DON'T HAVE ENOUGH INFORMATION TO MAKE AN INFORMED DECISION.
BUT I DO KNOW ONE THING.
WHATEVER MORLUN MAY THINK, I'M NOT PURE. AND THAT MAY BE MY ONE CHANCE TO BEAT HIM.
AND I INTEND TO DO JUST THAT.

SOUTHERN NEW YORK NUCLEAR POWER PLANT.

-- SO HE SAYS TO ME, "HOW CAN YOU WATCH THAT BABYLON 5 CRAP? I MEAN, IT TAKES FIVE YEARS TO PAY OFF SOMETHING YOU SEE IN YEAR ONE!" AND I SAID, "THAT'S EXACTLY IT!"
THAT'S GREAT, I --
CAUTION

OH, JEEZ...THAT'S THE REACTOR ALERT!
THIS IS THE PLANT SUPERVISOR...YOU ARE INSTRUCTED TO EVACUATE IMMEDIATELY...I REPEAT...EVACUATE THE FACILITIES AT ONCE...

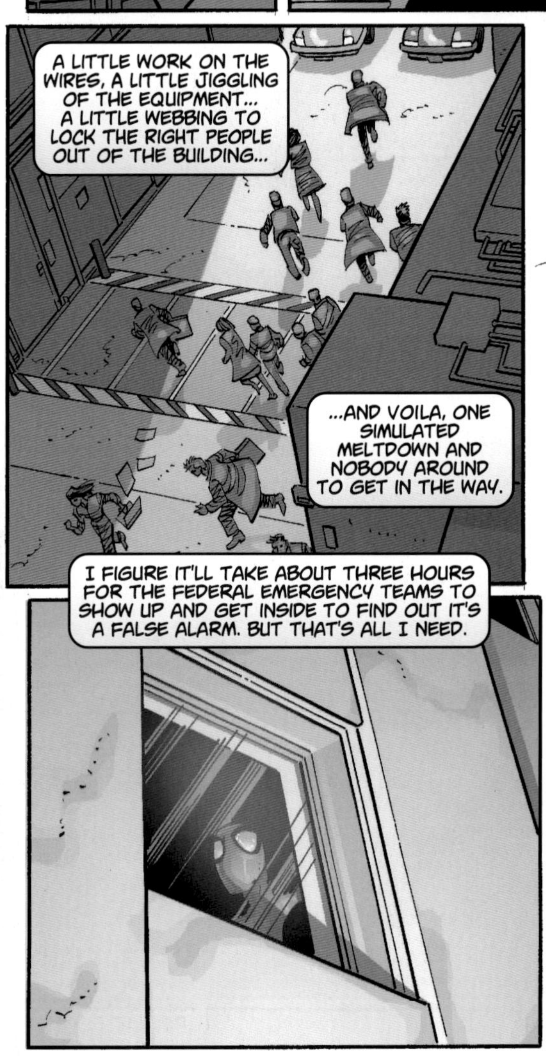
A LITTLE WORK ON THE WIRES, A LITTLE JIGGLING OF THE EQUIPMENT... A LITTLE WEBBING TO LOCK THE RIGHT PEOPLE OUT OF THE BUILDING...
...AND VOILA, ONE SIMULATED MELTDOWN AND NOBODY AROUND TO GET IN THE WAY.
I FIGURE IT'LL TAKE ABOUT THREE HOURS FOR THE FEDERAL EMERGENCY TEAMS TO SHOW UP AND GET INSIDE TO FIND OUT IT'S A FALSE ALARM. BUT THAT'S ALL I NEED.

WE'RE GONNA DANCE, YOU AND I, MORLUN. AND THIS IS GONNA END, RIGHT HERE, RIGHT NOW, FOREVER.
BECAUSE I'VE REACHED MY OWN CRITICAL MASS.
AND I'M TAKING YOU WITH ME.

The Amazing Spider-Man #35
COVER ARTWORK

I CAN FEEL MORLUN APPROACHING. ALMOST HERE.

AND I'M ALMOST OUT OF TIME. LITERALLY, FIGURATIVELY, AND IN EVERY OTHER SENSE OF THE WORD.
THERE ARE THINGS WE DO BECAUSE WE NEED TO, OR WE WANT TO, OR WE THINK WE REALLY OUGHT TO...
AND THERE ARE THINGS WE DO ONLY BECAUSE WE'RE DESPERATE AND THERE'S NO OTHER CHOICE. USUALLY THEY INVOLVE THE VERY REAL POSSIBILITY OF DYING.
THIS IS ONE OF THEM.

I CAN'T KID MYSELF. THIS COULD KILL ME EVERY BIT AS EFFECTIVELY AS MORLUN.

IF IT DOES, THEN AT LEAST I'LL DENY HIM THE PLEASURE OF FEEDING OFF THE SPIDER IN ME.
SECTOR 64

HEY! STOP!

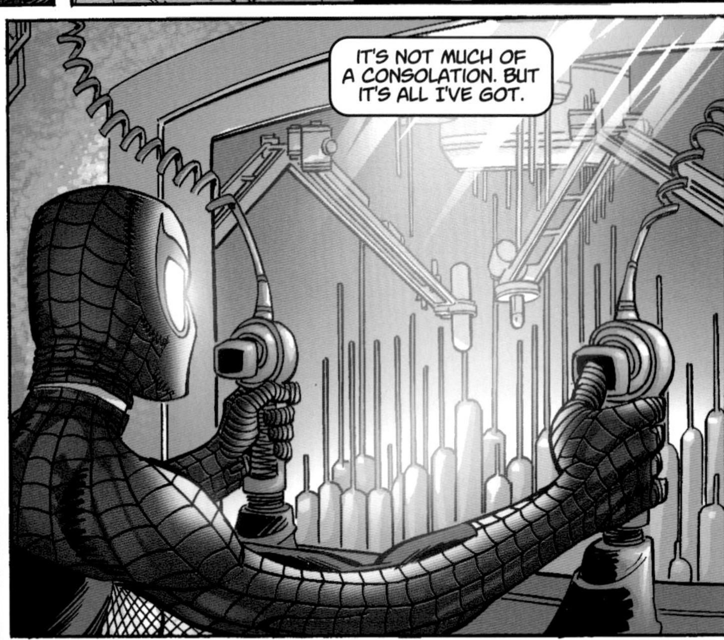
IT'S NOT MUCH OF A CONSOLATION. BUT IT'S ALL I'VE GOT.

HE'S INSIDE. WAIT FOR ME HERE.
TIME TO END THIS.
YES, MORLUN.

ORGANIC FLUID SUSPENSION COMPOUND. CHECK. BUFFERING COMPOUND. CHECK. ACCEPTABLE RADIATION LEVELS...
UNKNOWN. WHAT I CAN CONTROL IS THE AMOUNT OF FLUID I INJECT. TOO LITTLE AND IT WON'T HAVE ANY EFFECT. ASSUMING IT HAS ANY EFFECT AT ALL.

TOO MUCH AND IT'LL BOIL MY BLOODSTREAM, FRY MY INTERNAL ORGANS, MELT MY ARTERIES AND COOK MY HEART FASTER THAN AUNT MAY'S MICROWAVE.
SHHHHHTT
WHAT THE HELL... I NEVER WANTED TO LIVE FOREVER ANYWAY.
AAAAAAAGGGGHHH!
THE PAIN IS BEYOND DESCRIPTION.
BEYOND IMAGINATION.
EVERY NERVE IS ON FIRE.
MY HEART, READY TO BURST.
I CAN'T MOVE.
AND I SUDDENLY WONDER --
-- HAVE I JUST MADE A TERRIBLE MISTAKE?

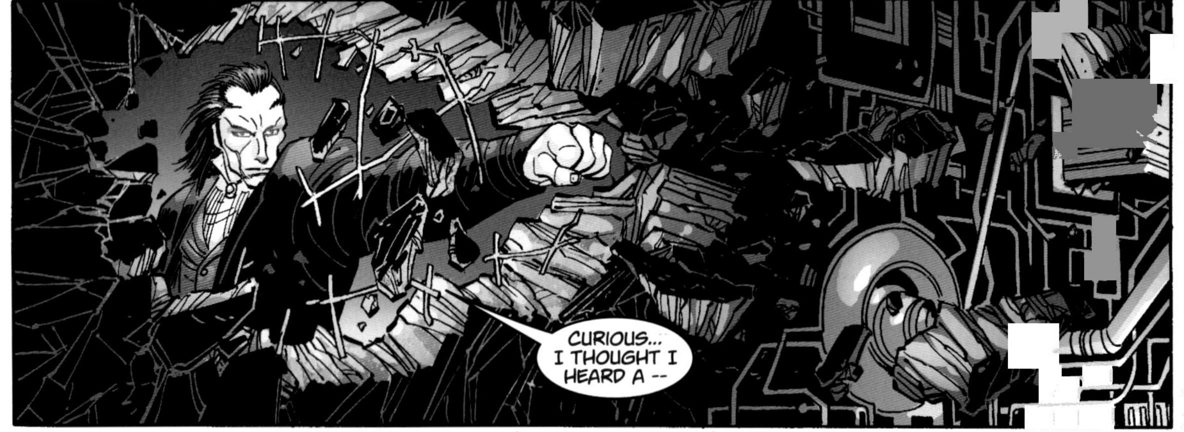
CURIOUS... I THOUGHT I HEARD A --

AH... IT WOULD APPEAR THAT I DID.

NOT THAT IT'LL MEAN MUCH TO YOU IN YOUR CURRENT CONDITION, BUT YOU'LL BE PLEASED TO KNOW THAT THE ENERGY I TAKE FROM YOU AT THE MOMENT OF YOUR DEATH, THE PURE SPIDER WITHIN YOU, WILL SUSTAIN ME FOR AT LEAST ANOTHER HUNDRED YEARS.

SO WHILE YOUR SACRIFICE WAS INEVITABLE AND UNWILLING...AT LEAST IT WAS IN A WORTHY CAUSE.

NOTHING TO SAY? UNTIL NOW YOU'VE BEEN TALKING FOR BOTH OF US. I DON'T HAVE YOUR SKILL. I HARDLY KNOW WHAT TO SAY. WELL, EXCEPT --

-- GOODBYE.

AAAAGGGHHHHHHH!

GET AWAY FROM ME!

I...I DON'T UNDERSTAND, WHAT --
TYPICAL, ISN'T IT?

JUST WHEN YOU THINK YOU KNOW SOMEONE...THEY SURPRISE YOU.
YOU WANTED TO FEED ON THE SPIDER IN ME, BECAUSE IT WAS PURE...RIGHT FROM THE SPIDER'S MOUTH SO TO SPEAK.
JUST ONE PROBLEM.
I MAY BE MANY THINGS... A SNAPPY DRESSER, A GOOD DANCER, AND OVERALL A HECK OF A NICE GUY ONCE YOU GET TO KNOW ME. BUT THERE'S ONE THING I'M NOT.

I'M NOT PURE.

THE SPIDER THAT BIT ME HAD BEEN SUBJECTED TO A MASSIVE DOSE OF RADIATION.
WHATEVER THE SPIDER HAD BEEN BEFORE THAT MOMENT, WHATEVER ITS INTENTIONS, IF ANY, WHATEVER POWERS IT CARRIED, IF ANY...ALL THAT CHANGED WITH THE RADIATION.
EZEKIEL ASKED WHICH CAME FIRST, THE CHICKEN OR THE EGG... THE RADIATION OR THE SPIDER? THE TOTEM OR THE ISOTOPE.
YOU KNOW WHAT I SAY?
I SAY IT DOESN'T MATTER TO WHO I AM, WHY I AM OR WHAT I AM.
MAYBE THE SPIDER FINALLY GOT SMART AND DECIDED TO EVOLVE TO THE NEXT LEVEL. MAYBE IT GOT STUPID AND WAS WHERE IT SHOULDN'T HAVE BEEN.
EITHER WAY, THE SPIDER AND THE RADIATION MET IN THE LAB, GOT HITCHED IN THE TEST TUBE, AND TOGETHER THEY PRODUCED... ME.
A CHILD OF THE SPIDER. FIRST COUSIN TO THE ATOM.
YOU CAN HANDLE THE FIRST. THAT'S WHAT YOU LIKE. THAT'S WHAT YOU FEED ON.
BUT RADIATION... AH, THAT'S A LITTLE HARDER TO SWALLOW, ISN'T IT?

AFTER THE FIRST DOSE, I ALWAYS WONDERED IF I COULD SUSTAIN ANOTHER DOSE... OR IF IT WOULD KILL ME. BUT I NEVER HAD A REASON TO TEST THE EQUATION. TO TAKE THAT CHANCE.
TILL NOW.
TILL YOU.
CONGRATULATIONS, SUNSHINE... YOU JUST REAPED THE WHIRLWIND.

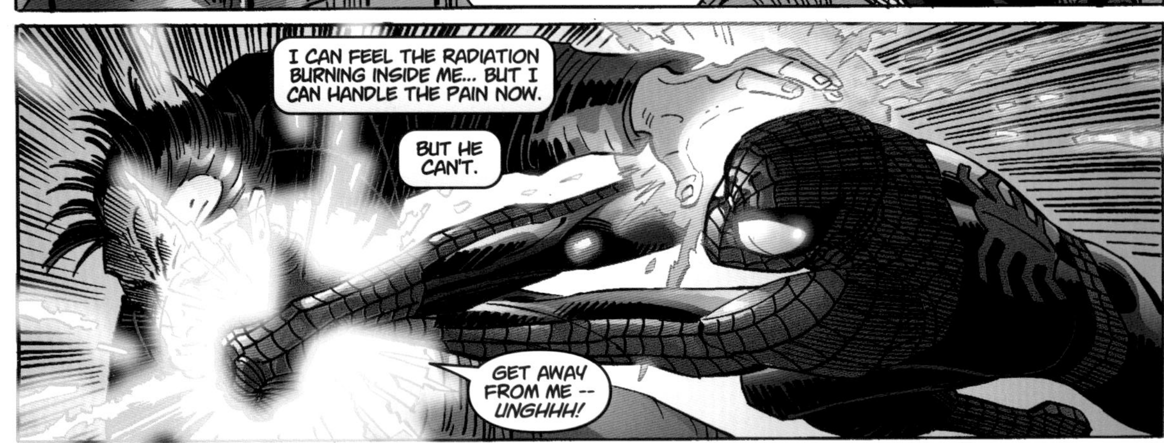
I CAN FEEL THE RADIATION BURNING INSIDE ME... BUT I CAN HANDLE THE PAIN NOW.
BUT HE CAN'T.
GET AWAY FROM ME -- UNGHHH!

EVERY TIME I HIT HIM, INSTEAD OF MY ENERGY, HE ABSORBS THE RADIATION AT THE POINT OF CONTACT.
CHOKE ON IT, BABY... CHOKE ON IT. 'CAUSE IT'S PAYBACK TIME.
HOW DOES IT FEEL TO BE ON THE OTHER SIDE OF THE IRRESISTIBLE FORCE, MORLUN?

HOW DOES IT FEEL TO BE PURSUED BY SOMEONE WHO ISN'T GOING TO BACK OFF OR GIVE UP?

HOW... DOES... IT... FEEL!?

YES! THAT ONE HURT HIM. THE RADIATION HAS WEAKENED HIM ENOUGH FOR MY PUNCHES TO GET THROUGH.

CAN'T LET HIM CATCH HIS BREATH. CAN'T LET HIM GET AWAY OR GET HIS STRENGTH BACK.
IT'S NOW OR NEVER. ONE CHANCE.
BUT THAT'S ALL I'VE EVER NEEDED.

ONE CHANCE TO TAKE IT TO THE WALL. ONE CHANCE TO STAND OR FALL ON MY OWN, LIVE OR DIE, SUCCEED OR FAIL.
NOT JUST FOR ME. FOR ALL THE PEOPLE HE'S HURT. FOR ALL THE PEOPLE HE'S KILLED.
FOR EZEKIEL.

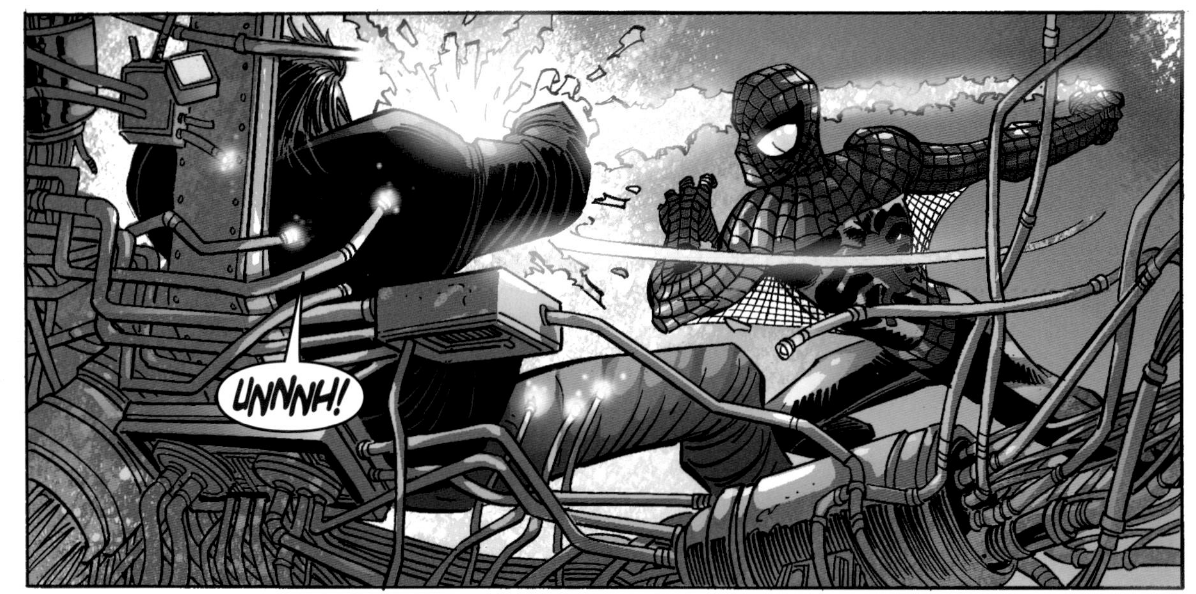
UNNNH!

PLEASE... NO MORE... I GIVE YOU MY WORD, I WILL LEAVE... I WILL NEVER RETURN --

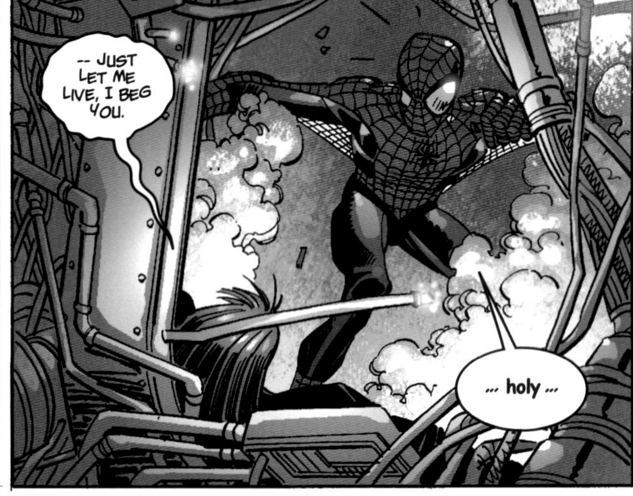
-- JUST LET ME LIVE, I BEG YOU.
... holy ...

PLEASE...
I CAN'T LET HIM GO... I CAN'T LET HIM GET HIS STRENGTH BACK... I STOPPED HIM ONCE, I DON'T KNOW IF I CAN DO IT AGAIN.

EVEN IF HE DOESN'T COME AFTER ME, HE'LL COME AFTER SOMEBODY ELSE.

HE'S VULNERABLE. HE CAN BE HURT. HE CAN BE KILLED. I STOP HIM RIGHT HERE, RIGHT NOW, OR HE GOES BACK TO KILLING.
GOD IN HEAVEN, PETER... HOW FAR ARE YOU PREPARED TO GO?

PLEASE --
I --
CLICK
WHAT...?
...DEX?
I QUIT.
NO!

THIS ISN'T... THIS CAN'T...DON'T YOU KNOW HOW OLD I AM...DON'T YOU KNOW HOW...

I WAS JUST HUNGRY, THAT'S ALL...IT WAS NOTHING PERSONAL...I WAS JUST... HUNGRY...

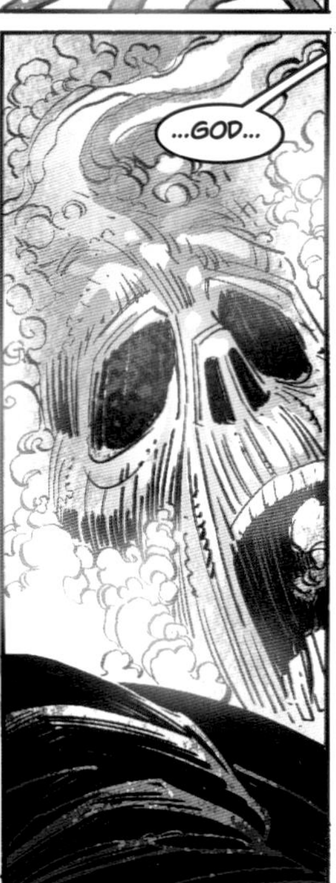
...GOD...

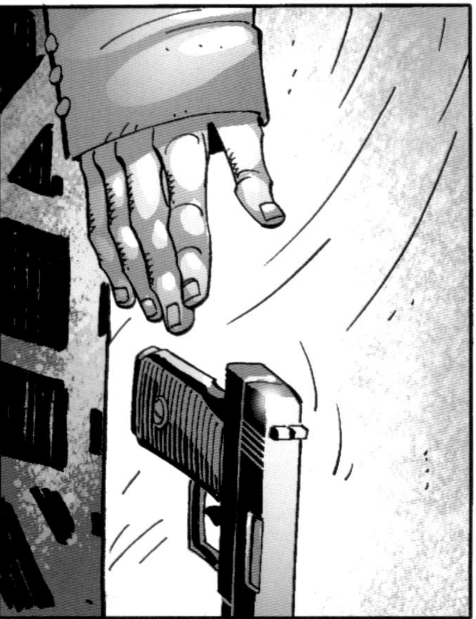

IT'S LIKE I TOLD YOU! THERE'S SOMEONE INSIDE! GET THE POLICE!
HAVE TO GET OUT OF HERE...NO WAY I CAN EVEN TRY TO EXPLAIN THIS TO ANYBODY.

IT'S NOT WHAT I WANTED.
NO. THAT'S NOT TRUE. IT IS WHAT I WANTED.

BUT AT THE END, WOULD I HAVE DONE IT?

I'LL NEVER KNOW.

BUT I'LL ALWAYS SUSPECT THE WORST.

...HUNH... HUNH...

...HUNH...
HUNH...

OUCH...
OW...
HEY.
YOU.

UHH...
HI.

HE HURT ME. HE HURT ME A LOT.

GET OUT. NEVER COME BACK. OR I WILL HURT YOU A THOUSAND TIMES WORSE THAN HE EVER DID.

...DING... DING...

...DING-DONG THE WITCH IS DEAD, WHICH OLD WITCH, THE WICKED WITCH...

"YES, SIR, THAT'S WHAT WE'VE FOUND...

"...THERE'S DEFINITELY BEEN A MELTDOWN... BUT I DON'T THINK IT'S EXACTLY WHAT YOU'RE WORRIED ABOUT..."

HELLO, GOD... THIS IS PETER PARKER. CAN I ASK A FAVOR?

I KNOW I'VE BEEN YOUR PERSONAL CAT TOY FOR THE LAST FEW YEARS...BUT CAN WE NOT DO THAT TO ME AGAIN FOR A WHILE?
NOT REAL LONG, I KNOW THE ODDS ON THAT ARE ABOUT ZERO...BUT JUST FOR A LITTLE WHILE.

SAY...FIFTY OR SIXTY YEARS? I MEAN, THAT'S NOT LONG IN YOUR TERMS, RIGHT?

JUST KIDDING, GOD... JUST KIDDING.

BUT I'LL BET YOU KNEW THAT, DIDN'T YOU?

SIMMS
WHEN MY KNEES STOP SHAKING, I GO TO CHECK ON EZEKIEL'S PLACE. I FIGURE SOMEBODY HAS TO TELL THEM HE'S GONE. TELL THEM HE STOOD UP, ANTED IN, AND WENT DOWN SWINGING.

BUT THE PLACE IS EMPTY. THE FURNITURE LOOKS LIKE IT WAS YANKED OUT FAST.

NOTHING. DID SOMEONE TELL THEM? DID THEY FIND OUT ON THEIR OWN? OR...

ARE YOU OUT THERE, EZEKIEL? DID YOU LAND ON YOUR FEET?
DO I NOT HAVE TO CARRY ONE MORE DEATH ON MY CONSCIENCE?

YOU'RE PRETTY CALM TO BE HANGING AROUND LIKE THIS WHEN EVERYBODY ELSE IS GONE. YOU'RE --
WAITAMINNIT...

SQUEAK

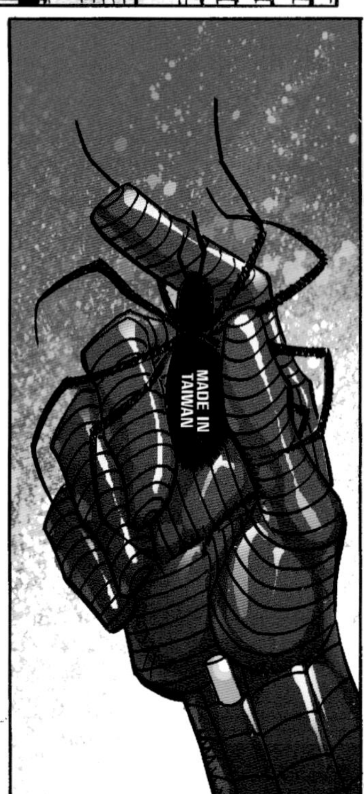
MADE IN TAIWAN

HEH...
HEH-HEH...

EZEKIEL!

DID YOU HEAR SOMETHING?
OF COURSE NOT.

NOW COME, WE HAVE PLACES TO BE, THINGS TO DO...

...PEOPLE TO HELP.
WHAT WAS THAT?

NOTHING... NOTHING AT ALL.

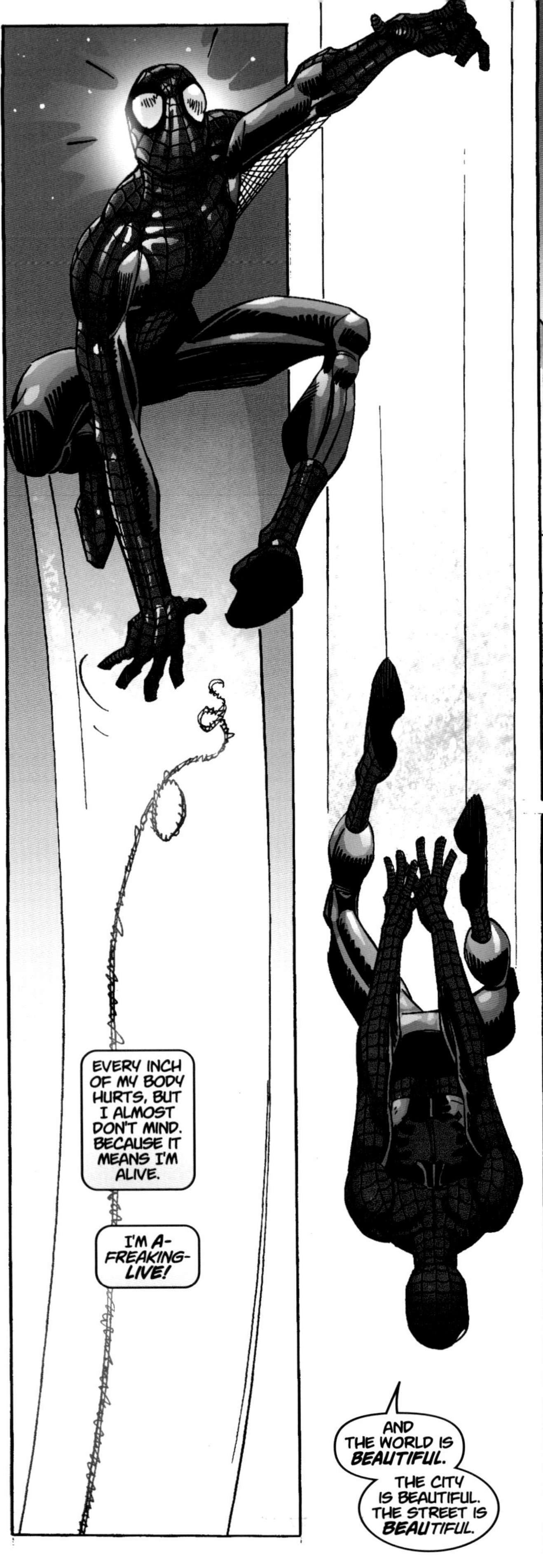
EVERY INCH OF MY BODY HURTS, BUT I ALMOST DON'T MIND. BECAUSE IT MEANS I'M ALIVE.
I'M A-FREAKING-LIVE!
AND THE WORLD IS BEAUTIFUL.
THE CITY IS BEAUTIFUL. THE STREET IS BEAUTIFUL.

EVEN YOU'RE BEAUTIFUL.
YEAH, AND MY WIFE SAYS I'M REALLY CUTE WHEN I'M ANGRY, SO TAKE A HIKE, YOU'RE BLOCKING TRAFFIC.

AND THE DELI IS BEAUTIFUL AND THE TRASH IS BEAUTIFUL AND THE HOOKERS ARE BEAUTIFUL --
-- WELL... KIND OF... WAITAMINNIT, IS THAT A GUY?
NUT.

MAN, THIS PLACE NEVER LOOKED SO GOOD. ACTUALLY, NO PLACE EVER LOOKED THIS GOOD.

OW... EVERYTHING HURTS...BUT AT LEAST I CAN FEEL THE RADIATION FLUSHING OUT OF MY SYSTEM THE SAME WAY IT DID AFTER THAT FIRST BITE.
SPEAKING OF WHICH...

...OH, MAN WAS THAT OVERDUE...

I'M GONNA SLEEP FOR A WEEK...THEN WHEN I'M TIRED OF THAT, I'LL GET SOME REST. THEN MAYBE A LITTLE MORE SLEEP, IF I'M UP TO IT.
IF NOT, THEN I'LL JUST NAP FOR A FEW WEEKS.

JUST LET ME LAST LONG ENOUGH TO HIT THE PILLOW...I'VE NEVER BEEN THIS TIRED BEFORE.
AT LEAST MY GOOD OLD SPIDEY-SENSE IS THERE TO LET ME KNOW IF ANYONE WHO MIGHT WANT TO HURT ME COMES IN, SO I CAN RELAX --

-- AND JUST SLEEEEEP...

2:32

3:15 PM

4:21

NOK
HELLO? PETER?

ARE YOU AWAKE? I CAN GO IF YOU'RE ASLEEP... I WAS JUST COMING BY TO PICK UP YOUR CLEANING LIKE I PROMISED...

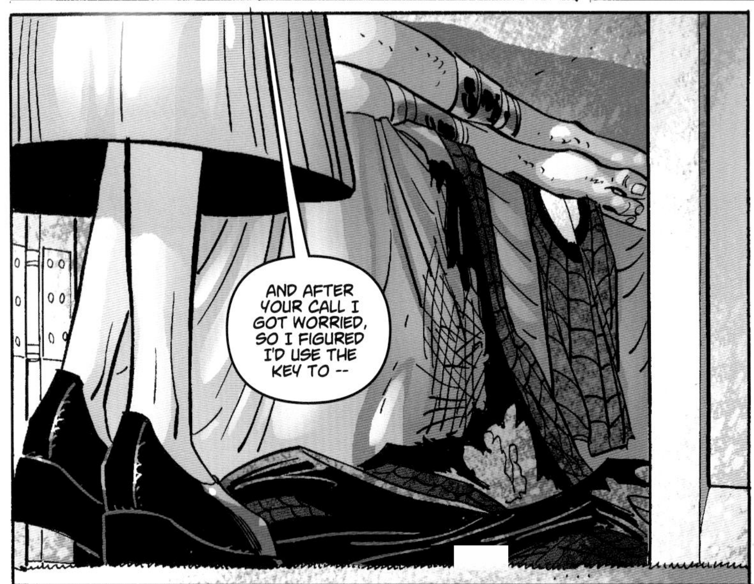
AND AFTER YOUR CALL I GOT WORRIED, SO I FIGURED I'D USE THE KEY TO --

-- TO...

To be continued in THE AMAZING SPIDER-MAN: REVELATIONS
(Volume 22 of the Ultimate Marvel Graphic Novel Collection)

ORIGINS...

Spider-Man

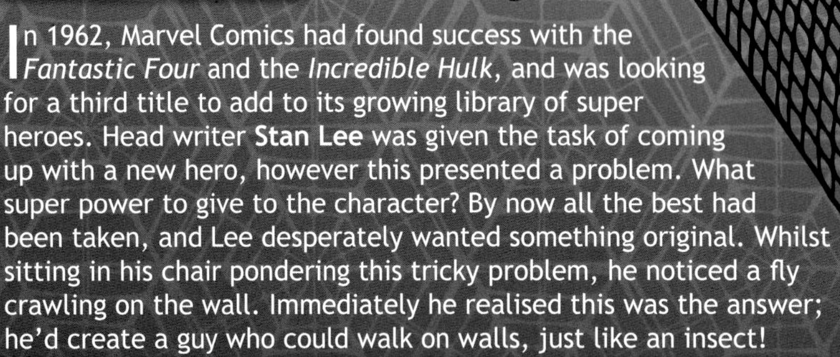

In 1962, Marvel Comics had found success with the *Fantastic Four* and the *Incredible Hulk*, and was looking for a third title to add to its growing library of super heroes. Head writer **Stan Lee** was given the task of coming up with a new hero, however this presented a problem. What super power to give to the character? By now all the best had been taken, and Lee desperately wanted something original. Whilst sitting in his chair pondering this tricky problem, he noticed a fly crawling on the wall. Immediately he realised this was the answer; he'd create a guy who could walk on walls, just like an insect!

According to Stan Lee, his next big problem was finding a name; "I figured, how about Insect-Man? And that didn't sound dramatic. Mosquito-Man? Nah. I went down the list. And when I got to Spider-Man, somehow it sounded dramatic. Spider-Man!"

In one of his boldest moves, Stan broke from tradition to make this new character a teenager. So far, all comic book Heroes had been adults and the only teens in comics were sidekicks, never the main man. By making Spider-Man's alter-ego Peter Parker a teenager he created a guy who the growing adolescent audience readers could instantly relate to.

Stan first approached **Jack Kirby** to help him create the look of the character, but decided that Jack's muscular super hero style wasn't quite right for a guy who, under the mask, was supposed to be an average teenager. His next port of call was another of Marvel's artists **Steve Ditko.** "Steve tended to draw things a little more realistically and more down to earth." Recalls Lee. "And he did it, and I really didn't interfere in what the costume looked like. Steve pretty much invented the costume himself." Along with the costume it was also Steve Ditko's idea to give Spider-Man his trademark web-shooters.

DID YOU KNOW?

Spidey still very nearly never made it off of the drawing board. The company's Chief Publisher Martin Goodman didn't want to use the character as he thought that people's fear of spiders would put them off, plus he doubted that anyone would really want to read a comic about a teenager.

However, Stan Lee was able to use Spidey when he heard that one of their titles, *Amazing Fantasy,* was going to be cancelled. Figuring that nobody would mind him using Spidey in a comic that was already on the way out, the webbed wonder made his debut in August 1962 in *Amazing Fantasy #15.*

The character proved an instant hit, especially with Marvel's new teenage audience, and it wasn't long before Spidey was given his own comic book series.

There are multiple Spider-Man titles released every month from Marvel, with core title, *The Amazing Spider-Man* the longest running at over 675 issues published to date.

A copy of Amazing Fantasy #15 recently sold for a record $1.1 million at auction!

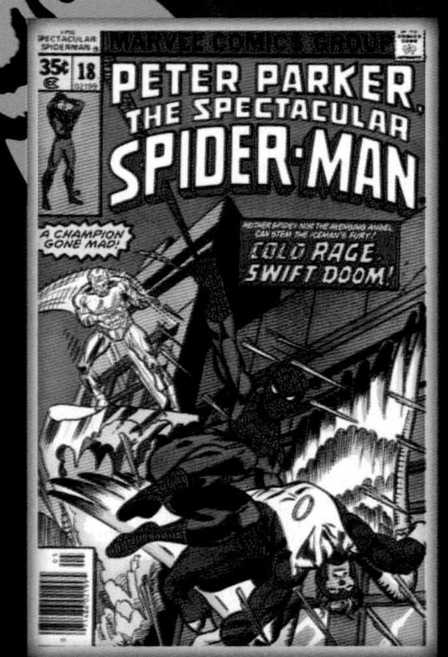

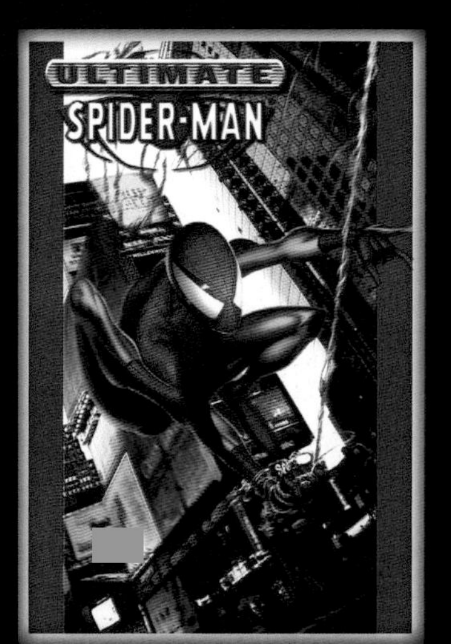

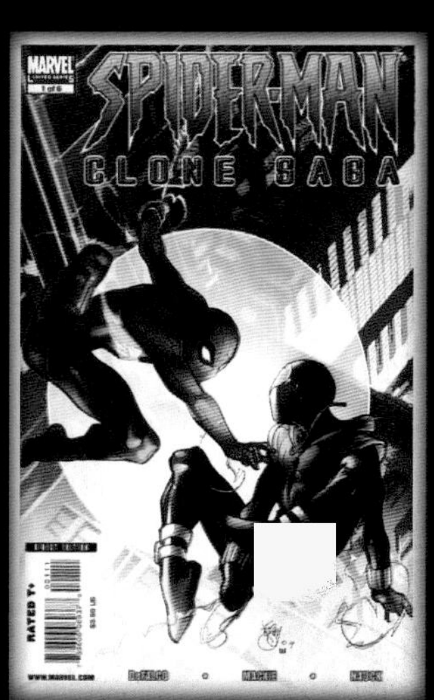

THE WRITER

How J. Michael Straczynski turned Spidey back into a top-seller!

John Michael Straczynski (or JMS to his fans)

FROM BOOM TO BUST

It's no understatement to say that the late 90's hadn't been kind to the US comic book industry. The boom period at the beginning of the decade, which saw some comics selling over 3 million copies, had turned into one of the biggest slumps the industry had ever seen. By 2000, Marvel had managed to pull itself out of a very rough phase of its corporate life, and was under new management. However, comic sales were still at an all time low. Recently appointed Editor-In-Chief **Joe Quesada** was acutely aware that a number of Marvel's most important comics had to be revamped to bring something new and original to the titles, in tune with the new decade. New blood was needed. In The Amazing Spider-Man's case, that meant **J Michael Straczynski.**

Child of the spider, first cousin to the atom...

A selection of Spidey's most beastly villains.

Best known as the creator of epic Sci-fi series *Babylon 5,* JMS had already had some experience writing a number of B5 spin-off comics, along with a couple of creator-owned series. With his TV script work paying the bills, JMS jumped at the chance to write Spider-Man and, in his own words, "feed his inner geek." Along with a lifelong love of the comic, JMS revelled in the creative freedom of comics. Filling panels with hundreds of extras or demolishing entire buildings cost nothing. This was a welcome relief from TV scripting, where everything had to be precisely budgeted down to the last dollar and cent.

SPIDER-MAN REBORN

JMS's plans for Spidey were revolutionary. Straczynski focused on an aspect of Spidey's origin, namely the unfortunate irradiated arachnid that bit him, and turned it on its head. Fans were instantly hooked on this intriguing new take on Spidey. Were his powers an accident of science or was there a more mystical reason behind them? This ability to take an aspect of an origin story and twist it in a way that reveals something new and intriguing about the character has become a trademark of Straczynski's comic work.

Along with the possible mystical roots to his origin, JMS also plays upon the idea of animal totems. Exploring the 'predator and prey' relationship between Spidey and his enemies inspired Stracynski to create a deadly new foe for the wall-crawler in the form of **Morlun.** Described as the ultimate hunter, this seemingly unstoppable energy vampire would prove to be one of the most dangerous creatures Spider-Man had ever had to fight.

Thanks to the level of trust Marvel had in his story-telling abilities, JMS was pretty much given free rein over what he could do with Spidey. Whilst still respecting the core values of the character, JMS took the wall-crawler in bold new directions. Over the next few years he would write some of the most original and exciting stories Spider-fans had ever read, firmly re-establishing the Amazing Spider-Man as a must-have comic.

THE ARTIST

John Romita Jr.

For John Romita Jr. (or JRJR as he's known to his fans), Spider-Man is like a member of the family. His father, John Romita Sr. was the artist who successfully replaced the web-slinger's co-creator Steve Ditko on Amazing Spider-Man back in 1966.

JRJR's own comicbook debut came in 1977, at the age of 21, when he illustrated *Chaos at the Coffee Bean!*, a six-page back-up story in *Amazing Spider-Man Annual #11.* Drawn while he was still a production assistant at Marvel, it led to his first regular series the following year. In collaboration with writers **David Michelinie** and **Bob Layton,** the young penciller produced a highly regarded run on *Iron Man* that continued until 1979. The trio reunited for another memorable run on the series in 1980, the same year JRJR produced his first X-Men work, illustrating *Uncanny X-Men Annual #4* and a single issue of the Marvel mutant's monthly title before following in his father's footsteps, taking over *Amazing Spider-Man* later that same year. He became the series' regular artist pretty much continuously through to 1984. Amongst the highlights of his run include his co-creation of the **Hobgoblin,** who was introduced in 1983's #238.

Never overshadowed by his father's legendary status, Romita Jr. was very much his own man with a developing style that put a modern twist on the traditional clean line work of artists from Romita Sr.'s generation. Towards the end of his tenure on *Amazing Spider-Man,* JRJR also began drawing *Uncanny X-Men.* The move to the title - by then a top-selling industry phenomenon - was a further boost to his skyrocketing career.

In 1988, his career took another upswing when he collaborated with writer **Ann Nocenti** and inker **Al Williamson** on *Daredevil.* This run on the street-level series introduced a major shift in the artist's technique. Gone was his earlier, more traditionally inclined art, replaced by a blockier, punchier style. "Visually, it went that way on its own." the artist remarked, "And I followed it. As I was getting gritty, somebody said, 'I like your stuff, it's getting gritty,' so I got grittier."

Much in demand, JRJR's subsequent credits are extensive. He has drawn virtually every Marvel hero and worked on almost all the House of Ideas' main titles. Discussing his approach to his work, he remarked, "My father once told me the artist's job is to draw out the words so that you should be able to follow the story without any dialogue. **Frank [Miller]** told me on several occasions that he had to force himself to put dialogue on certain pages of Man without Fear, which I took as the ultimate compliment. [Former Marvel/editor/writer] **Howard Mackie** and [famed writer/artist] **John Byrne** have said the same thing, and I do think it [storytelling] is my strongest point - better than my drafting, better than my actual art."

ARTIST'S GALLERY

Spider-Man

Drawing Marvel's friendly neighbourhood Spidey is merely a dream for many comic book artists, but for those who are skilled and lucky enough, their names will forever be linked to the history of the webbed-wonder...

ROGUE'S GALLERY

Call of the Wild

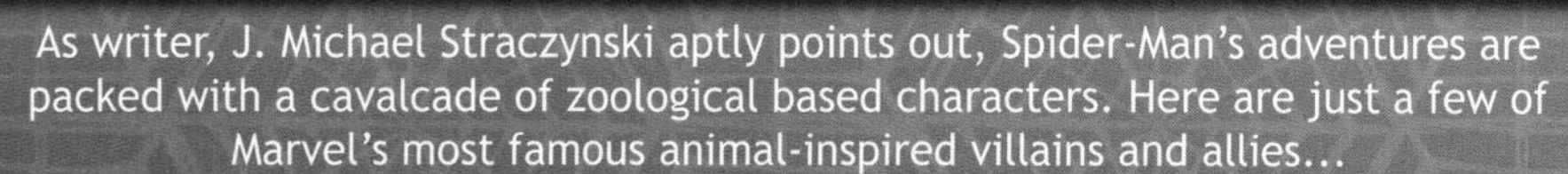

As writer, J. Michael Straczynski aptly points out, Spider-Man's adventures are packed with a cavalcade of zoological based characters. Here are just a few of Marvel's most famous animal-inspired villains and allies...

Chameleon
First Appearance
ASM#1 (1963)

Vulture
First Appearance
ASM#2 (1963)

Dr Octopus
First Appearance
ASM#3 (1963)

Lizard
First Appearance
ASM#6 (1963)

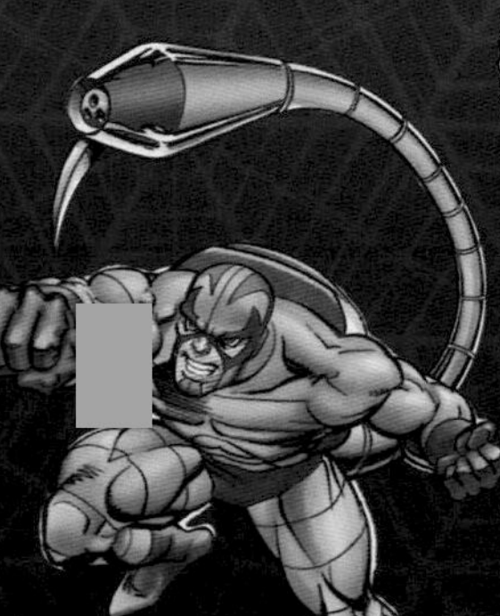

Scorpion
First Appearance
ASM#20 (1965)

Rhino
First Appearance
ASM#41 (1966)

Man-Wolf
First Appearance
ASM#124 (1973)

Jackal
First Appearance
ASM#129 (1974)

Tarantula
First Appearance
ASM#134 (1974)

Black Cat
First Appearance
ASM#194 (1979)

Puma
First Appearance
ASM#256 (1984)

FURTHER READING

If you've enjoyed the style and art in this graphic novel, you may be interested in exploring some of these books too.

*Other Marvel work by **J Michael Straczynski***

Amazing Spider-Man
Revelations
Volume 22 of the Ultimate Marvel Graphic Novels Collection
At the book shop:
ISBN: 9781904159094

Amazing Spider-Man
Life and Death Of Spiders
At the book shop:
ISBN: 9781904159315

Spider-Man
The Other
At the book shop:
ISBN: 9780785117650

*Other Marvel work with art by **John Romita Jr.***

Eternals
Volume 53 of the Ultimate Marvel Graphic Novels Collection
At the book shop:
ISBN: 9781905239573

World War Hulk
Volume 55 of the Ultimate Marvel Graphic Novels Collection
At the book shop:
ISBN: 9781905239771

Wolverine
Enemy Of The State
At the book shop:
ISBN: 9781905239290

SKETCHBOOK

J. SCOTT CAMPBELL

Cover artist ***J.Scott Campbell*** shares with us his draftboard sketches for ***The Amazing Spider-Man***...

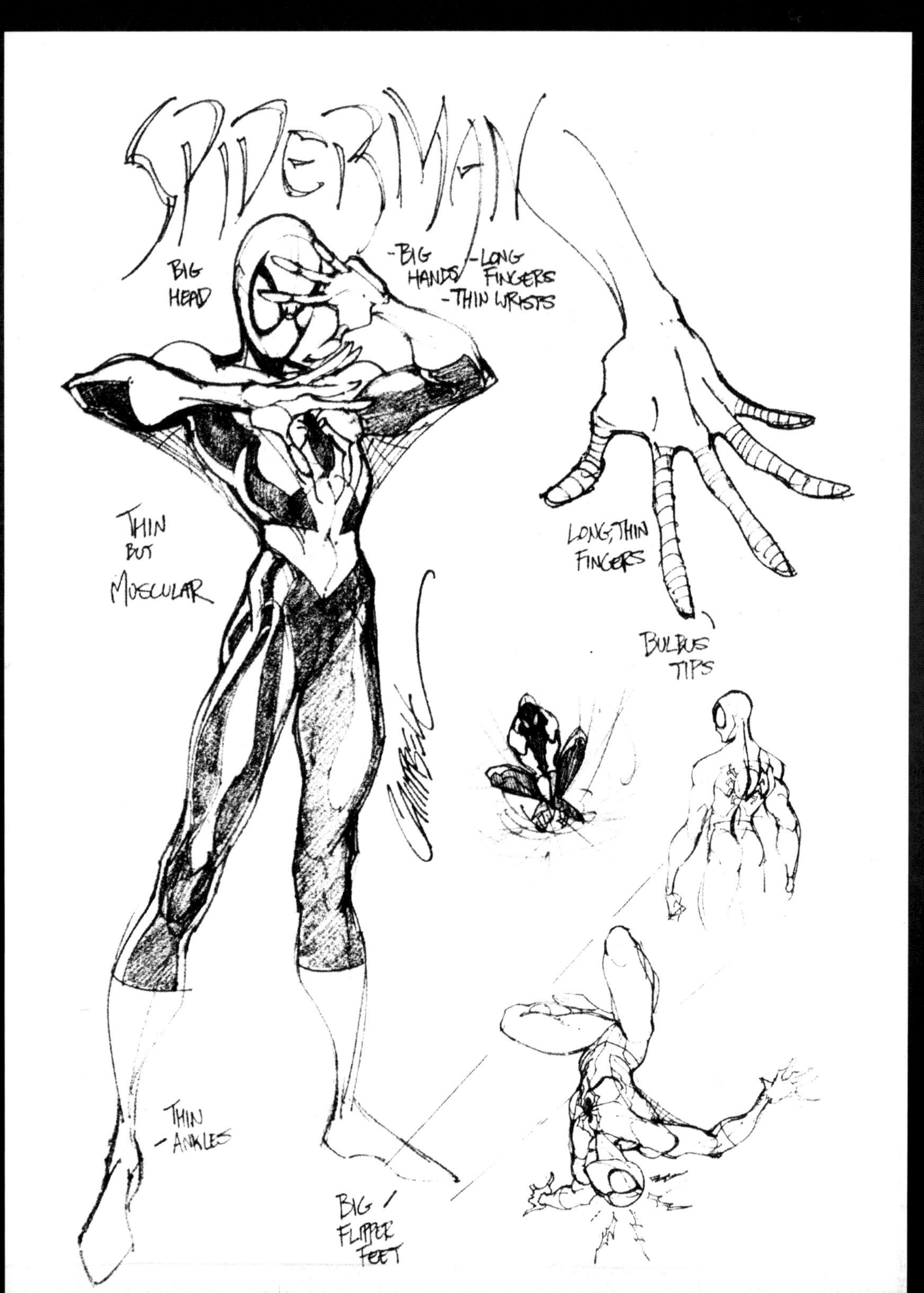

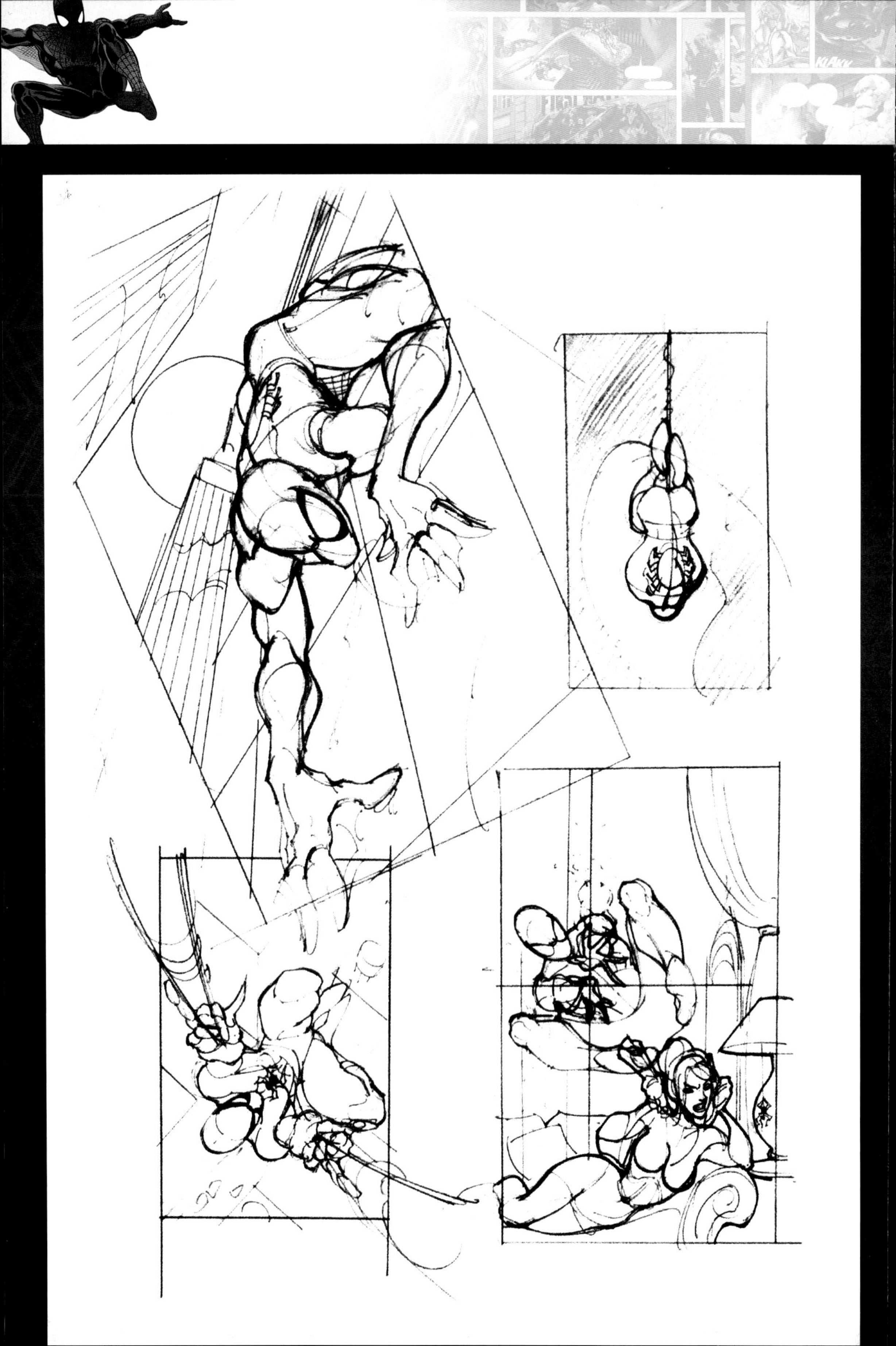

BUG
LIKE
KINDA
CREEPY
CAMPBELL 2000

PETER PARKER
MARY JANE
MYSTERIO
POC MARKS
DOC OC
8-EYES
SHAGGY "LOU FERRIGNO" HAIR + EYEBROWS
"AW YEAH!"
ME
HULK